Onwards and

Hereford United's promotion season 2005/2006

By Andy Compton of the Hereford Journal and Brian Goodwin of Bulls News

An ecstatic crowd of some 10,000 Hereford United fans witnessed the Bulls win an epic Play Off Final at the Walker's Stadium in Leicester on May 20th 2006. The 'Roy of the Rovers' style 3–2 extra time win against Halifax Town ended a nine year non-league stint for Hereford United. The result proved third time lucky for the club which had lost out in the play offs in the previous two seasons.

This book chronicles their successful play-off winning 2005/2006 season. It includes text from Bulls News featuring every league game and most cup games, along with pictures of every home game and a couple of away games. Virtually every player who played for the club that season is pictured, from popular striker Guy Ipoua to loan signing Matt Bailey.

This book pays tribute to the management and team which returned Hereford United to the Football League. We hope you enjoy looking back on the season as much as we've looked back on these games while compiling it."

Andrew Compton and Brian Goodwin.

Nationwide Conference: Final League Standing 2005–2006

			--- home ---					--- away ---						
		Pld	W	D	L	F	A	W	D	L	F	A	GD	Pts
1.	Accrington Stanley	42	16	3	2	38	17	12	4	5	38	28	31	91
2.	Hereford United	42	11	7	3	30	14	11	7	3	29	19	26	80
3.	Grays Athletic	42	7	9	5	46	32	14	4	3	48	23	39	76
4.	Halifax Town	42	14	6	1	31	11	7	6	8	24	29	15	75
5.	Morecambe	42	15	4	2	44	17	7	4	10	24	24	27	74
6.	Stevenage Borough	42	15	3	3	38	15	4	9	8	24	32	15	69
7.	Exeter City	42	11	3	7	41	22	7	6	8	24	26	17	63
8.	York City	42	10	5	6	36	26	7	7	7	27	22	15	63
9.	Burton Albion	42	8	7	6	23	21	8	5	8	27	31	-2	60
10.	Dagenham and Redbridge	42	8	4	9	31	32	8	6	7	32	27	4	58
11.	Woking	42	8	7	6	30	20	6	7	8	28	27	11	56
12.	Cambridge United	42	11	6	4	35	25	4	4	13	16	32	-6	55
13.	Aldershot Town	42	10	4	7	30	30	6	2	13	31	44	-13	54
14.	Canvey Island	42	6	8	7	23	27	7	4	10	24	31	-11	51
15.	Kidderminster Harriers	42	8	5	8	21	27	5	6	10	18	28	-16	50
16.	Gravesend and Northfleet	42	8	4	9	25	25	5	6	10	20	32	-12	49
17.	Crawley Town	42	9	4	8	27	22	3	7	11	21	33	-7	47
18.	Altrincham	42	7	5	9	25	30	3	6	12	15	41	-31	41
19.	Southport	42	7	3	11	24	38	3	7	11	12	30	-32	40
20.	Forest Green Rovers	42	7	7	7	31	27	1	7	13	18	35	-13	38
21.	Tamworth	42	4	10	7	17	23	4	4	13	15	40	-31	38
22.	Scarborough	42	4	7	10	24	30	5	3	13	16	36	-26	37

Published by Andy Compton

Photographs of Hereford v Altrincham and 2006–2007 season squad pictures were taken by Steve Niblett and Kidderminster Harriers v Hereford United pictures reproduced by kind permission of the Express and Star. All other pictures taken by Andy Compton.

Reports of the Gravesend, Southport and Morecambe games by Ex Landlord. Reports of the Halifax home game and Kington Town and Cambridge City away games were written by Kevin Goodwin. All other reports by Brian Goodwin.

ISBN 0 9554666-0-1 (978-0-9554666-0-1)

Printed by Print Plus
126 Widemarsh Street
Hereford HR4 9HN

Hereford United v Scarborough.
Guy Ipoua scores the second goal against Scarborough as 'keeper Leigh Walker attempts to anticipate the header.

Hereford United v Scarborough, 13 August 2005. Report by Brian Goodwin

Second half onslaught sinks Scarborough

After a goalless first half, Hereford United ripped Scarborough apart at Edgar Street with four goals after the break. Graham Turner handed debuts to Dean Beckwith, Alex Jeannin, Andy Ferrell, Stacy Coldicott, Jon Brady and star of the show, Guy Ipoua.

Scarborough enjoyed the opening spell with some prolonged possession although it was the hosts who threatened first when Jeannin's dangerous cross from the left was headed behind. Clear cut chances were hard to come by in this tough opening half, which saw two very determined teams foil each others attacks.

It was United who almost took the lead midway through the half after some good build up play. Ferrell played the ball into Ipoua who, with his back to his marker, flicked the ball around the defender, and sprinted through on goal. The Cameroonian did everything right and fired beyond the reach of Leigh Walker in the Boro goal, but was denied by the near post.

Ryan Green had a good opportunity when his run into the box from the right was picked out with a good pass, but he took an extra touch forcing him wide. The Welshman managed to cut the ball back across goal where Adam Stansfield attempted to force the ball over the line but the danger was cleared.

Scarborough's first chance did not come until just in the second half, but they will look back on this missed opportunity and perhaps mark that as a changing point in the game. Jeannin mis-judged a left wing delivery, allowing it to go over his head and Ashley Lyth was behind him to direct a header goalwards. Craig Mawson came to Jeannin's rescue and plucked the ball out of the air to keep the score line level.

Ipoua, whose power and pace caused problems for the Seadog's defence all afternoon, hit a Green cross against the cross bar, triggering a goalmouth scramble where Stansfield also had a good chance to net. Then, United were incensed as they were denied what appeared to be a fairly clear cut penalty. Jeannin went to head a cross at the far post, and in doing so was caught on the head by a flying Scarborough foot. The referee, though, amazingly ignored the claims and allowed play to continue, even though Jeannin was on the floor with a head injury.

Finally though, The Bulls did get their breakthrough and it was a debutant who opened his Hereford account. Jeannin took a corner from the right and up leapt Beckwith at the near post to glance a header towards goals. It flew beyond Walker and hit the underside of the bar before bouncing into the gaping net in front of a packed Meadow End.

From then on it was all one way traffic as the floodgates opened and the Bulls did not hesitate in taking full advantage. Other than a one off attack for the visitors, in which Mawson did well to come out and deny Mark Quayle, The Bulls dominated fully and played some fantastic football much to the delight of the Edgar Street crowd of 3105.

Hereford's second goal followed five minutes later when Green knocked the ball back to Brady on the right flank and he swung in an inch perfect cross to Ipoua. Ipoua held off the challenge from his marker and met the ball with a diving header, sending the ball underneath the diving goalkeeper.

Rob Purdie was introduced in Brady's place, he had been booked, with fifteen minutes remaining and Carey-Bertram replaced Stansfield on eighty three minutes, two minutes before the Bulls made it three. The Bulls broke quickly after a Boro corner through Green. He raced forward before releasing a pass to Ipoua, but his shot was pushed away. Luckily though, it fell right into the path of Green, who'd continued his run, and he hammered the ball into the back of an empty net.

Ipoua received a standing ovation as he left the field of play, and Craig Stanley took his place. In the final minute the rout was completed in a move that involved all three of the substitutes. Rob Purdie burst forward before sliding a pass into the path of Stanley's run, just in the penalty box, but his low show was pushed away by Walker, but Carey-Bertram was on hand to fire home to make it 4-0 to the Bulls.

There were many happy faces seen leaving Edgar Street this afternoon, having witnessed what was a very good opening day of the season for United. The team was organised in defence and looked full of ideas going forward. After a tough first half, Hereford broke down their opponents and went on to

Hereford United v Scarborough.
Hereford United defender Tamika Mkandawire out jumps prolific Scarborough forward Mark Quayle.

Hereford United v Scarborough.
NOT THIS TIME... Scarborough defender Tony Hackworth just beats Hereford's Dean Beckwith to a cross.

Hereford United v Scarborough
Hereford United defender Dean Beckwith heads clear despite the efforts of Scarborough forward Jermaine Palmer.

demolish them, sending out a stern message to the rest of the Conference. They will be eager to follow this result up though, when they make the trip to Cambridge United on Tuesday night, in front of Sky TV cameras.

HUFC: Mawson, James, Mkandawire, Beckwith, Green, Jeannin, Coldicott, Ferrell, Brady, Stansfield, Ipoua. Subs: Blewitt, Brown, Purdie, Stanley, Carey-Bertram.

SFC: Walker, Elebert, Weaver, Baker, Lyth, Bishop, Hackworth, Clark, Nicholson, Quayle, Wake. Subs: Foot, Pecora, Redfearn, Eccles, Palmer.

Cambridge United v Hereford United, 16 August 2005. Report by Brian Goodwin

Defensive mistake costs Bulls

Hereford United fell to their first defeat of the season last night away at the Abbey Stadium live on Sky TV. Cambridge United took the lead before half time and went on to win 2-1, after Guy Ipoua had netted an equaliser for the visitors. Graham Turner named, as expected, an unchanged side following the first day victory.

The U's started well with John Turner forcing a save from Mawson after his strike partner, Folawiyo Onibuje, flicked on a cross. Onibuje was at the heart of most of the hosts attacks and caused endless problems for the Hereford defence with his physical presence and power. The Bulls had a good penalty claim early on when Ipoua headed Brady's cross and the ball appeared to hit a defenders arm but the referee waved away the shouts.

David Bridges headed over after attacking a cross from the left with a late run while Dean Beckwith nodded Alex Jeannin's corner over. Hereford began to take a hold of the game and it was Andy Ferrell who went close after a good break from defence. Man of the match Ryan Green collected a cross field ball and swung the ball into the near post where

Ferrell beat the 'keeper to the ball but his shot was off target. Adam Stansfield headed wide before Brady went as close as anyone had came. Tamika Mkandawire broke up a prolonged Cambridge spell and brought the ball out of defence, played a one-two and the delivered a cross for Brady, who volleyed towards the far post but the ball bounced inches wide.

However, moments before the half time break, the hosts were in front. Tony James, for some reason known only to him, attempted to dribble the ball out of defence between two opposing players. Inevitably, he was dispossessed and The U's had fired the ball beyond Craig Mawson before you knew it. Steven Smith fired the ball in from twenty yards to make it 1-0. Ipoua attempted to level things up before the break but his shot on the turn was off target.

Stacey Coldicott saw his volley held after Brady's corner was only half cleared at the start of the second half before David Chick was booked for hand ball on the edge of his own penalty area. Brady was unable to take advantage of the chance and shot wide though. Turner made his first change with Rob Purdie replacing Ferrell early on in the half and within five minutes Hereford had equalised, not before Onibuje had headed wide and Brady had fired over from twenty yards.

The Bulls won a corner and on hand at the far post was Ipoua who powered a header into the bottom corner from Jeannin's deep cross. The goal spurred the Bulls on and for a while it looked as though there would only be one winner. Green played a neat ball down the flank to Ipoua, who held up play before finding Stansfield in the box. Stansfield laid it on for Green who hammered a left footed drive towards the top corner, but it was superbly kept out by Darren Behcet. He dropped the ball though and Brady was quickly on the scene to hit a rebound but Behcet completed a great double save.

Beckwith picked out Jeannin on the left with a good long ball and Ipoua was unfortunate not to get on the end of the Frenchman's cross as it was turned behind by Chick. Then, against the run of play, The Us found themselves in front once again. A high ball into the box was headed away by Mkandawire but fell nicely for Turner. His volleyed shot was closed down by James, but it fell kindly to Bridges who managed to slip the ball in from a tight angle. Coldicott was replaced by Danny Carey-Bertram in attempt to change fortunes by the Hereford manager.

There was more poor play by Hereford at the back and they almost gifted Cambridge a third goal. Sub Parys Okai disposed a defender and delivered a perfect cross for Onibuje at the far post but he managed to head wide while unmarked at the far post. The Whites were given one final chance in injury time when Ipoua was felled on the edge of the box having already skinned two opponents. Brady hit the free kick off the wall and it fell to Mkandawire, but he scooped a volley over the bar from three yards.

Having not built on the home success of the first day of the season will be very disappointing for Hereford. They will be even more frustrated with the defeat as it was not really deserved. The Bulls will feel that they did enough to gain at least a draw from the game but in the end a defensive mistake has cost them dearly. There is, though, plenty of time to make up any lost ground following this 2-1 defeat in front of a gate of 2,924.

HUFC Team: Mawson, James, Mkandawire, Beckwith, Jeannin, Green, Coldicott, Ferrell, Brady, Ipoua, Stansfield. Subs: Blewitt, Brown, Purdie, Stanley, Carey-Bertram.

CUFC Team: Behcet, Gleeson, Peters, Duncan, Chick, Smith, Bridges, Quinton, Angel, Turner, Onibuje. Subs: Okai, Daniels, Nolan, Robbins, Duffy.

United jump to second

Hereford United came away from The Broadfield Stadium with an eventually comfortable 2-0 victory against Crawley Town. A generally poor first half lacked any real skill from either side, as the long ball tactic was adopted by both providing a frustrating spectacle.

Graham Turner made one change from the side that has started the last two games with Rob Purdie being promoted from the bench, swapping places with Andy Ferrell. Otherwise, The Bulls were unchanged.

Hereford started well and created an early opening after a good run to the corner by Adam Stansfield, who crossed to the far post where Ryan Green laid the ball on to Jon Brady, but his effort was drilled over the bar. Stansfield tested 'keeper Phil Smith with a shot on the turn but Smith gathered easily before Richard Hodgson was booked for the hosts. Jamie Cade went close to opening the scoring for Crawley after a free kick from the left led to a scramble in the box before Cade forced it wide with the goal gaping.

Stansfield supplied his strike partner with a ball through on goal but Ipoua was forced wide by Smith but, having rounded the goalkeeper, had to cut back as he fired a tame effort wide. Ipoua then danced his way between two defenders and saw his effort deflected safely into the 'keepers arms while, at the other end, Steve Burton smashed a twenty five yard effort towards goal that needed the fingertips of Craig Mawson to push it over the bar.

Burton then was gifted a chance to put the home side in front but was denied by the post after Stacy Coldicott was dispossessed and the ball was flicked through to Burton. Brady attempted an overhead kick from Stansfield's cross after Tamika Mkandawire had found the attacker, but it was off target as the half came to a close.

The game had faded towards the end of the first half and it also lacked incident until Hereford opened the scoring after fifty eight minutes. On one of the few occasions that The Bulls actually managed to get the ball on the ground and put together a series of passes, they tore Crawley apart and took the lead. Coldicott provided the defining pass after United had broke down the right, finding the run of Green in behind the defence and he slid the ball across the face of goal to give Ipoua the simple task of firing Hereford into the lead.

Brady then had a great chance to double the advantage but his bullet header at the near post, from Ipoua's cross, was the wrong side of the post. Craig Stanley was introduced in place of Coldicott with twenty minutes to go while ex-Bulls Danny Davidson came on for Crawley. Brady's free kick caused all sorts of problems in the home sides penalty area with two crucial blocks keeping the score line down before a break saw a good chance for Burton, but he smashed his volley wide.

First half sub, Stuart Douglas, shot on the turn but it was wide before Davidson almost equalised from the edge of the box. His low shot came off the foot of Tony James and totally wrong footed 'keeper Mawson. However, he managed to readjust quickly and throw himself down to tip the ball around the post for a corner. He then had to be alert as the corner dropped in the danger-zone and he was quickly down once again to claim.

Purdie fired over the bar from twenty yards after man of the match Stansfield had past two defenders and cut back for him before Danny Carey-Bertram replaced Ipoua. The sub was involved in the build up to the second goal for Hereford, as he won them a corner on the right in the eighty third minute. Smith made a mess of clearing Alex Jeannin's corner and the ball fell into the path of Mkandawire who fired into the roof of the net for 2-0.

Stansfield was blatantly brought down as United broke late on and Ian Simpemba saw yellow for this act. The resulting free kick, in injury time, was worked down the right where Stansfield eventually crossed for Jeannin but he fired wide at the far post.

Although the eventual outcome was reasonably comfortable for Hereford, there were stages in the game where the tactics appeared to be all wrong and it was difficult to see where a goal would come from. However, when decided to get the ball down it paid off. The first time they did this in the second half resulted in the opening goal. The overall performance was not the best, but the 300 or so travelling supporters in a crowd of 1,842 will be more than happy with the result.

HUFC Team: Mawson, Mkandawire, James, Beckwith, Jeannin, Green, Coldicott, Purdie, Brady, Stansfield, Ipoua. Subs: Blewitt, Brown, Ferrell, Stanley, Carey-Bertram.

CTFC: Smith, Judge, Simpemba, Hodgson, Elam, Wormwull, Cade, Blackburn, Woozley, Jenkins, Burton. Subs: Ward, Opinel, Douglas, Davidson, Brown.

Hereford United v Grays Athletic, 27 August 2005. Report by Brian Goodwin

James Gifts Grays Victory

Hereford United put in a poor performance at Edgar Street this afternoon and fell to their second defeat of the season. Newly promoted Grays Athletic looked a dangerous outfit that should do well in this league. However, they did not have to work too hard to gain victory today.

Manager Graham Turner kept the faith in the same side that defeated Crawley Town a week ago with Rob Purdie keeping his place in the middle of the park. The only change was on the bench where Darren Blewitt failed to recover from a foot injury and so Graham Evans took his place. Andy Ferrell was on the bench again; it is thought that he did not play today because Turner wants him to start against Tamworth, who will be a more physical side than Grays.

Hereford started brightly and were in control for the first quarter of an hour before disaster struck once again for Tony James. Jon Brady had fired an early shot over the bar before Guy Ipoua set up his strike partner Adam Stansfield with a ball in behind the defence, but Stansfield hit the side netting.

With fifteen minutes on the clock, Craig Mawson rolled the ball out to skipper James,

Hereford United v Grays Athletic

Grays goalkeeper Ashley Bayes leaps to punch clear under pressure from team mate Joe Bruce and Hereford United's Adam Stansfield.

Hereford United v Grays Athletic
Hereford United goalkeeper Craig Mawson punches clear while airborne with team mate Tamika Mkandawire and Grays defender Cam Mawer.

who had been impressive until then, in the Hereford defence, and James was quickly closed down. Instead of clearing the ball to safety, or knocking it to Dean Beckwith who had given James an option to his left, he attempted to dribble the ball out of defence. He was soon tackled and Tony Battersby made no mistake in smashing the ball into the bottom corner beyond the reach of Mawson. This is not the first time that James has stupidly lost the ball in defence this season, leading to a goal for the opposition.

It was down hill for Hereford from then on, as heads dropped and Grays got a foot hold in the game. Chances were few and far between for the remainder of the half; Dennis Oli saw a shot after a Grays break saved by Mawson while Ipoua's header from Ryan Green's cross was no trouble for Ashley Bayes in the visitors goal. On the stroke of half time Brady came close again with a free kick that was not too far away from the intended top corner.

A far more eventful second period started with Stuart Thurgood curling an effort just wide. Brady was close yet again to equalising soon after; his half volley was just inches over the cross bar from twenty yards. John Nutter's left footed free kick on the flank bypassed everyone in the Hereford box although Gary Hooper almost connected with a header at the far post.

Rob Purdie spread play to Green on the right and the Welshman burst towards the box was ended as he was fouled twenty yards out. Alex Jeannin's free kick hit the wall though and a Grays burst forward ended with man of the match Dean Beckwith heading a dangerous cross behind. Craig Stanley replaced the injured Rob Purdie with a hour gone. Stansfield headed Jeannin's free kick goal bound but once again Bayes wasn't troubled, while at the other end a misunderstanding between James and Beckwith resulted in a good recovering challenge from the latter.

This may have been the final straw for Turner and within minutes he replaced his captain, James, with Danny Carey-Bertram as The Bulls reverted to a 4-4-2 formation with Carey-Bertram on the left wing. Green kept the score at 1-0 when he cleared a header off the line following a corner before John Martin hit the post from close range, when he really should have doubled the visitors advantage. United broke quickly but Carey-Bertram's cross was cleared, triggering a counter attack for Athletic. Substitute Jamie Slabber beat the offside trap and had a clear run on goal, but shot wide with Tamika Mkandawire putting in a last ditch tackle to put him off.

Hereford had their best spell of the game after this with some good chances to level things up, but thanks to Bayes they failed to do so. Brady's corner was knocked on before

Mkandawire's shot was blocked. It fell to Stansfield and his shot was blocked too before Beckwith volleyed over. At the other end a double goal line clearance by Green saved United further embarrassment before Hereford felt sure they should have had a penalty. A shot by Carey-Bertram, after

Hereford United v Grays Athletic
Hereford United captain Tony James watched Grays striker Tony Battersby celebrate his goal with team mates.

Stanley's free kick, hit the arm of a defender but the referee dismissed appeals.

After hitting the defenders hand, the ball fell back to Stanley, who saw his drive go out for a corner. Mkandawire came close with a low left footed drive from twenty five yards, that almost caught Bayes unaware. However, the ex-Woking stopper scrambled across his line to push it out for a corner. Carey-Bertram then went close at the game came to an end after some good, patient, build-up play, when Stansfield knocked a short ball to him in the box but once again Bayes tipped the ball wide.

Hereford failed to make use of the five added minutes at the end and were punished right at the end. Martin had hit the side netting already before a cross in from the right was tapped in from close range by Hooper much to the delight of the 57 away fans. A fair number of the home fans in a crowd of 2,997, rose to their feet and left the stadium before the end of the game.

All in all, this was a poor performance by Hereford and they will defiantly not be able to afford many more of that sort if they are to meet their ambition of automatic promotion this season. There were far too many players on the pitch today who, for one reason or another, did not seem to put the effort required in. Although short term memories of this result may be forgotten with a win at Tamworth on Monday, it may prove more costly come the end of the season.

HUFC Team: Mawson, Mkandawire, James, Beckwith, Jeannin, Green, Coldicott, Purdie, Brady, Stansfield, Ipoua. Subs: Brown, Stanley, Ferrell, Carey-Bertram, Evans.

GAFC: Bayes, Bruce, Stuart, Mawer, Nutter, Hooper, Thurgood, Martin, Poole, Oli, Battersby. Subs: Brennan, Matthews, Kightly, Ayres, Slabber.

Hereford United v Grays Athletic
Grays goalscorer Tony Battersby challenges Hereford defender Dean Beckwith for the ball.

Not Quite The Silence of the Lamb

Today's Bank Holiday Monday saw Hereford United travel to The Lamb, home of Tamworth, as they attempted to get back on track following Saturday's disappointing defeat at the hands of Grays Athletic. A far more superior performance was needed than that of two days ago, and Graham Turner made a point from the start by making five changes to the starting eleven. Introduced were Wayne Brown, making a first Bulls start, Andy Ferrell, Craig Stanley, Danny Carey-Bertram and Darren Blewitt, also making a first start for United.

However, The Bulls' were still at sixes and sevens early on, and it was no surprise The Lambs had the better of the opening twenty minutes. Striker Julian Alsop went closest in the period for the hosts, but his far post header was narrowly wide from a Hugh McAuley cross. Against the run of play, though, the visitors took the lead; and it was the first time they'd really troubled Tamworth's back line. Adam Stansfield raced away down the right, managing to, just, speed beyond Graham Ward and lofting a cross to the far post where Alex Jeannin, who'd bust a gut to get forward from defence, managed to meet the strikers delivery and power a forceful header into the near top corner in front of the delighted away contingent.

From then on, the match was a scrappy encounter as neither side was able to take control of the game, or the ball for that matter. Possession switched between both and no notable goal scoring opportunities before the half time whistle sounded.

However, five minutes after the interval the home side were again keeping goalie Brown alert, though McAuley's effort, from Bob Taylor's chest down, was over the cross bar. The Bull's must have treated this as a wake up call of sorts, as they sprang into life. Ferrell released Stansfield with a defence splitting pass but Stansfield was unable to hit the target and Tamworth escaped.' Keeper James Dormand then pulled off a save of the highest quality as he denied Jon Brady a fabulous goal, which was destined for the top corner from outside of the box, but Dormand flung himself across his goal and just managed to tip the ball away with an outstretched finger or two.

Tamworth put in a reaction to United's couple of chances but big Mat Redmile just missed the target with a strong header from a left sided corner, much to the relief of the large away following before Bob Taylor almost netted what would have probably been a deserved equaliser. The ball was played into his feet, and with his back to goal the experienced marks man skilfully turned and hit an instinctive shot on the turn, but, again, the strike failed to hit the target.

Tempers flared with just four minutes remaining, and both sides finished the game with ten men. Ryan Green was involved in an incident, in which he appeared to be fouled, but the referee allowed play to go on and no free kick was given. It was the assistant referee on the near side that seemed to keep an eye on things between Green and Ward, as the players squared up to each other as play continued. After a large brawl between players on both sides, and a lengthy discussion between the referee and his assistant, Green was brandished the red card. The home crowd cheered, but were quickly silenced as their man, Ward, was shown the same card.

They were silenced further as the full time whistle was blown with the score at 1-0 to Hereford. The performance was better than against Grays, but still not to the standard that will be required if United are to meet their ambitions come May. It's three extra points on the board though and a clean sheet so, in that respect, Turner couldn't have asked for much more from his side following Saturday.

HUFC: Brown, Green, Beckwith, James, Blewitt, Jeannin, Brady, Stanley, Ferrell, Stansfield, Carey-Bertram. Subs: Coldicott, Purdie, Mawson, Evans, Ipoua.

TFC: Dormand, Smith, Redmile, Brown, Ward, Alsop, McAuley, Storer, Stamps, Jackson, Taylor. Subs: Turner , Hollis, Bampton, Gayle, Whitman.

Hereford United v Altrincham, 3 September 2005. Report by Brian Goodwin

Goalless draw frustrates Bulls

Hereford United dominated throughout but failed to get a decisive breakthrough against Altrincham this afternoon at Edgar Street. Graham Turner made only one forced change to the side that defeated Tamworth on Bank Holiday Monday; Rob Purdie stepped into the place of the suspended Ryan Green at right wing back. There was a return for Tamika Mkandawire, but only to the subs bench and also making the bench was long term absentee Jamie Pitman.

Hereford started well but it was The Robins who first went close when, after some good build up play, Colin Potts saw his effort from the edge of the box tipped around the post by Wayne Brown. Adam Stansfield had a good chance to break the deadlock with Hereford's first real opening, when his striker partner Danny Carey-Bertram turned well and spotted the run of Stansfield but he was foiled by the on rushing Stuart Coburn when one on one with the 'keeper.

Hereford United v Altrincham.

Hereford United's loan signing Darren Blewitt just loses out to the Altrincham goalkeeper as Dean Beckwith looks on. Blewitt came on loan to the Bulls from West Ham United.

Hereford United v Altrincham.
The Altrincham goalkeeper collects a cross under pressure from Hereford United's Darren Blewitt.

Hereford United v Altrincham.
Hereford defender Tony James heads clear to midfielder Craig Stanley watched by Jon Brady.

Stansfield again forced Coburn into a good save, this time when he headed Alex Jeannin's corner towards the bottom corner. Coburn failed to gather it the first time but was quick to grab hold of it again before a Hereford player got there. Stansfield finally got the ball in the back of the net but his celebrations were cut short by a raised flag on the far side for offside. After a good move Craig Stanley had slammed a shot low towards the goal and Stansfield was quick to get a foot on it and divert it past Coburn, but was adjudged to be offside.

Tempers rose soon after when Collin Little squared up to Dean Beckwith and seemed to push Beckwith in the chest right in front of the dugouts. The referee missed the incident but was informed of events by the fourth official. Beckwith was booked first and the yellow card followed for Little, much to the annoyance of Bulls coach John Trewick, who seemed to think, along with many others, that Little should have been sent off.

It was not long before the referee made another important decision which once again meant that Altrincham kept eleven players on the pitch. Stansfield got the better of Gary Talbot when battling for a long ball over the top and Stansfield got ahead of the defender, only to be pulled to the ground just outside of the box. Talbot was the last defender and still the referee failed to produce a red card. Jon Brady struck the resulting free kick but it was tipped over by Coburn.

Purdie, who played very well as stand in wing back, crossed to man of the match Stansfield before half time but the header was saved. However, before the break a Bulls counter attack saw Brady just miss a cross from the right before Jeannin cracked the ball back into the middle, where Stansfield didn't fully connect when a yard out.

Hereford started the second period with more possession but again unable to find an opening. Stansfield cut back to Stanley, but his tame effort was blocked before Jeannin fed the ball down the flank for Stansfield, but Carey-Bertram was just inches away from connecting with the pass across the goal face. Carey-Bertram managed to get a shot away from the next cross, courtesy of Purdie, but his deflected effort rebounded off the cross bar.

Brady was replaced with twenty minutes to go because of a hamstring injury, and so Graham Evans made his first home appearance. Stanley was at the start and finish of another Hereford move, but after Purdie had found Ferrell and he'd laid the ball out to Stanley, the low drive flashed wide. Stacey Coldicott replaced the injured Alex Jeannin with fifteen minutes left and Ferrell moved to left wing back. Stansfield created one last good chance out of nothing for United when he tackled a defender on the left, cut into the box but was denied at the near post by Coburn.

All in all, United will be frustrated with the result as they really should have won this game. In truth, Altrincham rarely troubled the home side but did look to be a decent outfit. If they continue to perform like that they should have no problems in staying in this division although they may need a little more firepower in attack. There were many good

Hereford United manager Graham Turner sees the funny side of a refereeing decision while his assistant John Trewick looks bemused!

performances from Hereford players in what was probably their second best performance of the season. It was just unfortunate that they couldn't find that killer touch that was needed so badly.

HUFC: Brown, James, Blewitt, Beckwith, Jeannin, Purdie, Ferrell, Stanley, Brady, Carey-Bertram, Stansfield. Subs: Mkandawire, Mawson, Evans, Coldicott, Pitman

AFC: Coburn, Rose, Band, Talbot, Adams, Potts, Owen, Hawes, Olsen, Williams, Little. Subs: Acton, Maddox, Chalmers, Melling, Hendley.

Stevenage Borough v Hereford United, 10 September 2005. Report by Brian Goodwin

Third Consecutive Clean Sheet

The clash between two of the Conference favourites ended 0-0 at Broadhall Way this afternoon, but it will probably be Hereford who will be the most disappointed in not taking all three points. Stevenage were reduced to ten men in injury time at the end of the game and only really forced Wayne Brown into one save, as he kept his impressive record of not conceding as yet.

United faced a mini injury crisis before the game and it was only Alex Jeannin out of the pre-match doubts who made the starting eleven. Adam Stansfield missed out allowing Graham Evans to deputise. Guy Ipoua is still struggling with a hamstring problem and Simon Travis remains a couple of weeks away from fitness. Jamie Pitman was once again on the bench, as was Tamika Mkandawire. Rob Purdie continued in the place of the suspended Ryan Green.

Hereford had the better of the early stages but failed to create a lot in the way of goal scoring opportunities. Danny Carey-Bertram should have opened the scoring midway through the first half but having done the hard work on latching onto a through ball and rounding 'keeper Alan Julian, his effort was tame and cleared off the line by a recovering defender.

Graham Evans, replaced at half time by Pitman, went close with a snap shot from the edge of the box in The Bulls only other notable chance of the half, following a spell of possession from Boro but they did not capitalise. The other notable incident came when Anthony Elding blatantly pushed Brown into his own goal and then, when they both got to their feet, over-reacted to what he claimed was a raised hand by the 'keeper. Both were booked.

Former Boro favourite Jon Brady fired a free-kick over the bar early in the second period and then forced Julian into a spectacular diving save with a left footed shot from twenty yards out. At the other end Stevenage had a great chance of snatching a goal when substitute Simon Weatherstone saw his first time shot hit a defender and fall kindly to Darryn Stamp, but was denied brilliantly by Brown, from just six yards out with the goal gaping.

Hereford were to go close twice more, firstly with Craig Stanley, following a brilliant move through the midfield, but once again Julian denied him and then from man of the match Dean Beckwith, who smashed a rocket of a shot inches wide of the upright from twenty five yards. Tony James was also impressive at the back alongside Darren Blewitt.

In the second of four added minutes at the end of the game, Carey-Bertram was released with a ball over the head of the last man Ronnie Henry but Henry managed to catch up and up-end Carey-Bertram twenty yards out. It could not be said for sure whether Henry was the last man, but he'd already seen a yellow card and was shown another, leaving Stevenage to battle out the remaining moments a man down. Brady came close to winning it with the resulting free kick, but Julian kept Boro level for a final time.

Both sides will be happy that they have not conceded and United would have probably taken a draw before the game, so all in all this is not a bad result for the visitors. However, Hereford cannot afford to drop many more points with Exeter doing so well at the top. United find themselves in tenth place. A bonus is that they haven't conceded in three games, but Hereford haven't scored in more than four hours of football now.

Hereford United v Morecambe (*report opposite*)
TRUE GRIT... Hereford United goalscorer Andy Ferrell.

HUFC Team: Brown, James, Blewitt, Beckwith, Purdie, Jeannin, Ferrell, Stanley, Brady, Evans, Carey-Bertram. Subs: Mkandawire, Mawson, Pitman, Coldicott, Williams.

SBFC: Julian, Warner, Gregory, Hocking, Henry, Nurse, Quinn, Bulman, Boyd, Stamp, Elding. Subs: Laker, Gore, Williams, Weatherstone, Berquez.

Hereford United v Morecambe, 17 September 2005. Report by Brian Goodwin

Bulls get back on track

Hereford United kept their sixth clean sheet in eight games to secure a 1-0 home victory against Morecambe this afternoon. The Shrimps were not lacking in confidence having travelled to Edgar Street on the back of a 5-2 defeat of Aldershot and caused some problems for the mean Hereford defence, but the back three excelled throughout and Wayne Browns goal was rarely endangered.

Jamie Pitman took the place of the injured Graham Evans in the injury struck United side meaning Jon Brady moved into attack alongside Danny Carey-Bertram. The injury list, not helped by the suspension of Ryan Green, is so hefty at the moment that Graham Turner could only name four substitutes.

Michael Twiss pounded a shot wide firstly for The Reds after Garry Thompson had forced his way through a couple of challenges while Pitman fired wide at the other end. Alex Jeannin brought down Twiss on the very edge of the box, after a rather poor start to the game, and received a yellow card, the first of many in the game, for his actions.

Hereford United v Morecambe
Hereford's Dean Beckwith flicks on a corner for team mate Darren Blewitt.

Darren Blewitt was booked for a nasty challenge on Thompson before United had a

Hereford United v Morecambe

Hereford United midfielder Craig Stanley takes on Morecambe full back Jim Bentley.

Hereford goalkeeper Wayne Brown collects a cross.

good penalty shout waved away. Andy Ferrell crossed for Craig Stanley and his goal bound header was clearly deflected away by the hand of a defender, but not in the view of the referee. Dean Beckwith placed a superb through ball into the run of Stanley as The Bulls created the best chance of the half. Stanley's run took him beyond the defence and his shot from twenty five yards had beaten the on rushing Ryan Robinson, but it curled just inches wide.

Wayne Curtis forced Brown, who is yet to concede for Hereford, in to a wonderful one handed save moments before the deadlock was broken when he smashed a shot in from the right of the penalty box. Jeannin was the creator, when he beat his man and saw his centre deflected to the edge of the box where Ferrell was on hand to fire a perfectly placed volley into the bottom corner with just four minutes left of the half. Before the half was over, Chris Blackburn was booked for diving.

Thompson almost levelled things up soon after the restart but his right footed effort went inches wide of the far post. Chances were hard to come by in the early stages of the second period, but Hereford did manage to force a number of corners. Stanley had a shot blocked after being picked out by Brady before the Australian was replaced by Andy Williams. Blackburn received his marching orders following a foul on Jeannin down the left, with seven minutes remaining, in which Beckwith was booked and Tamika Mkandawire replaced Carey-Bertram.

The three points were important today against a tough side, who started the day in fifth position. Although work still needs to be done on the attacking side, the cause has not been helped by the absence of Guy Ipoua, Adam Stansfield and Graham Evans. At the other end though, Hereford are looking very safe indeed. Man of the match today was Tony James, who put in an immaculate performance as did Pitman. Both seemed to be everywhere in the defence today; whenever a tackle was needed one of the two were there to make it. In front of 2,422, this pleasing result moves The Bulls up three places, to seventh, in the Conference table.

HUFC: Brown, James, Blewitt, Beckwith, Jeannin, Purdie, Pitman, Ferrell, Stanley, Brady, Carey-Bertram. Subs: Mawson, Mkandawire, Gwynne, Williams.

MFC: Robinson, Blackburn, Bentley, Kempson, Howard, Thompson, Perkins, Hunter, Curtis, O'Connor, Twiss. Subs: Walmsely, Carlton, Kelly, Stringfellow, Davis.

Hereford United v Gravesend & Northfleet, 20 September 2005. Report by Brian Goodwin

Late lapse proves costly

Hereford United were unable to hold onto the lead and dropped two points late on against Gravesend & Northfleet this evening at Edgar Street. The draw will seem even more frustrating when the news of Exeter's defeat and York's draw find its way to Hereford.

With Ryan Green back from suspension and Jon Brady suffering with a groin strain, Graham Turner made just the one change to the starting eleven, with Green replacing Brady. Rob Purdie moved into attack alongside Danny Carey-Bertram and Green took his usual position at right wing back. Graham Evans recovered from injury and was named on the bench for The Bulls.

Gravesend started the game brightly, with three corners in the first couple of minutes, the first of which came with just seconds gone when Dean Beckwith misplaced a headed pass back. Alex Jeannin was busy on the left for Hereford and had it not been for a good cut out by a defender, Purdie would have had an easy tap in following Jeannin's cross early on. Carey-Bertram fired wide when he was

Hereford v Gravesend.
Craig Stanley beats Gravesend 'keeper Craig Holloway to put the Bulls 1-0 up.

Hereford v Gravesend.
Hereford players Danny Carey-Bertram, Andy Ferrell, Craig Stanley and Rob Purdie celebrate Stanley's goal against Gravesend.

presented with the ball following a short head back from a defender, but he fired wide of the far post from twenty yards.

Purdie was the supplier this time for Jeannin when he split the defence with a pass to Jeannin, attacking from the left, and he saw his effort go narrowly wide of the far post. Craig Stanley was quick to close down, and dispossess a defender on the half way line but Carey-Bertram should have done better when presented with a good chance after Green's early cross. Almost immediately at the other end, Beckwith had to make a brilliant recovering tackle to deny Charlie McDonald. Before the half was over, Purdie forced Craig Holloway into a good save and Jay Saunders volleyed just over for the visitors.

Hereford came out for the second half with renewed energy and looked more dangerous. Purdie was not to far away from Carey-Bertram's cross just moments after the restart and, after a counter attack, Jeannin was just unable to reach Purdie's through ball before 'keeper Holloway. However, with eight minutes of the half gone, The Bulls broke the deadlock. Purdie played a superb through ball inside the left back for Carey-Bertram, and he centred for Stanley who swept the ball home from close range.

Jeannin smashed a training ground free-kick regime inches over from twenty five yards soon after the opener, but The Fleet, from then on, began to get back into the game and started causing United some problems. Bobby Bowry forced Wayne Brown into a wonderful save with a volley from outside of the box, which the 'keeper managed to tip onto the crossbar. A good spell for Gravesend followed, with a number of corners from which they looked threatening. Brown was again called upon to make a good save after a scramble in the box, and then somehow, when the ball fell to Saunders, he managed to fire over from point blank range.

Hereford v Gravesend.
Gravesend's players turn to celebrate Bobby Bowry's equaliser.

Hereford v Gravesend.
Gravesend's Charlie MacDonald shields the ball from Hereford's Darren Blewitt.

It was then United's turn to put some pressure on the visitors, but they failed to make anything of four successive corners before disaster struck and Gravesend equalised. A corner was awarded when man of the match Beckwith blocked a cross and Graham Turner took the opportunity to make his first change, sacrificing a striker for a defender. Carey-Bertram, who had just been booked, was replaced by Mkandawire but the reinforcement failed to work as Gravesend scored from the corner. The ball fell in the box and Bowry hit an instinctive shot that flew through a crowd of players and into the back of the net, much to the delight of the travelling support of 38. Brady was brought on in a last ditch attempt to retake the lead. Purdie crossed for Pitman, but his out stretched boot directed the ball just wide and Mkandawire headed just wide in the last minute from a Purdie corner.

It proved to be an extremely frustrating night for Hereford and they will be most disappointed, especially considering other results, at having conceded so late on. Turner must be regretting his decision to make a change at such a crucial point in the game; it is often said that you should never make a sub when there's a corner to defend. It was evident that Gravesend were pressing and Hereford needed some fresh ideas with around twenty minutes to go, and it has to be wondered why a change wasn't made before.

The gap has been closed between the leaders and now eight placed Hereford following the draw, in front of 2,396, but Hereford are still to string together two victories this season, something that they will want to put right much sooner than later. The next game is away to Halifax next Saturday.

HUFC: Brown, James, Blewitt, Beckwith, Jeannin, Green, Pitman, Stanley, Ferrell, Purdie, Carey-Bertram. Subs: Mkandawire, Mawson, Brady, Williams, Evans.

GNFC: Holloway, Protheroe, Graham-Smith, McCarthy, Daniel Glozier, Slatter, Saunders, Bowry, Jackson, MacDonald, Drury. Subs: Aaron Kerr, Gooding, Surey, Omoyinmi, Grant.

Halifax Town v Hereford United, 24 September 2005. Report by Brian Goodwin

Third loss sees drop to ninth

Hereford United fell to a disappointing third defeat of the season away against Halifax Town this afternoon. The Bulls were handed a pre-match boost with the news that top scorer Guy Ipoua had recovered from a hamstring injury, but his comeback was short lived as he was replaced with a recurrence of the injury after fifteen minutes.

By that time though, the visitors were already in front following a three-piece move. Craig Stanley played a delightful pass over to Alex Jeannin on the left flank, and his equally excellent volleyed cross was perfect for the run of Danny Carey-Bertram, who managed to lose his marker, and he headed in at the far post.

Graham Turner had made two changes from the side that drew with Gravesend on Tuesday; Jon Brady was promoted to the starting line up in place of Jamie Pitman and Guy Ipoua replaced Rob Purdie. Purdie was soon back in the action though, when he took the injured Ipoua's place.

Dean Beckwith was booked early on for pulling John Grant's shirt, kick starting a feud between the two that would continue until Beckwith was replaced soon after half time, when he almost received his marching orders. Sugden got the better of Beckwith on ten minutes, and crossed for ex-Bull John Grant, but his shot on the turn went over. Hereford tried hard in attack, but created little and the only other save of the half for Ian Dunbavin was from a Stanely shot that he didn't have to move for.

Wayne Brown had to be alert in United's goal though, to deny a low shot from Grant after some good link up play with Sugden while Carey-Bertram fired wide on the stroke of half time. Halifax made one change at half time seeing Craig Midgley come on for Waybe Jacobs and The Shaymen took charge of the game almost instantly.

After an over hit corner, Danny Forrest returned the ball into the danger zone, where Grant once again got the better of Beckwith and converted from close range with just two minutes of the half gone. After this, Hereford's heads seemed to drop and they never really looked like getting back into the game. The second half performance was not good to say the least, and in some departments lacked effort.

Purdie fired over after Andy Ferrell had hooked a pass over the defence in a rare attempt from United before Grant shot over once again for Town. Tamika Mkandawire took to the field in Beckwith's place after he was nearly booked again, on 57 minutes and Pitman replaced the ineffective Brady, who took a knock, with twenty minutes to go.

The Shaymen almost took the lead on the counter attack after Mkandawire had over hit a cross, but a brilliant save from man of the match Brown kept the scores level, after Grant had played Sugden through. Adam Quinn had seen a header tipped over by Brown with around ten minutes to go, but once again United conceded late on. With four minutes to go, Grant was played through on goal only to be brilliantly denied by Brown, yet again, but substitute Chris Senior was first to the rebound and fired home the winner.

Chants of "what a load of rubbish" from some in the away end pretty much summed up the second half from The Bulls and there was a confrontation between some "supporters" and Jon Brady as the players left the field. There is a lot of work to be done if Hereford want to achieve their goal this season, and maybe a switch of formation would aid this.

HUFC: Brown, James, Blewitt, Beckwith, Jeannin, Green, Ferrell, Stanley, Brady, Carey-Bertram, Ipoua. Subs: Mkandawire, Mawson, Pitman, Evans, Purdie.

HTFC: Dunbavin, Haslam, Quinn, Ingram, Wright, Forrest, Thompson, Foster, Jacobs, Sugden, Grant. Subs: Leister, Bowler, Midgley, Young, Senior.

Aldershot Town v Hereford United, 27 September 2005. Report by Brian Goodwin

Bulls win at The Rec again

Hereford United continued their tradition of taking all three points from Aldershot Town as the rivals clashed once again at The Recreation Ground last night. It is the fifth time that the two sides have met in the Conference and Hereford boast a 100% record.

The sides were, yet again, equally matched and it was no surprise that just one goal was enough to separate the sides, although both looked as though they could have added to the score line. Graham Turner made some much needed changes following the unacceptable performance at Halifax on the weekend. Skipper Tony James was sacrificed to accommodate a change of formation, to 4-4-2. Dean Beckwith was absent meaning Tamika Mkandawire and Darren Blewitt paired up at centre back. Rob Purdie was reintroduced to the side on the left wing and new loan signing Matt Bailey partnered Danny Carey-Bertram in attack.

And the change of tactics paid dividends almost immediately for United. Even before everyone had time to make their way into the ground, the visitors had broken the deadlock. A long ball direct from the kick off resulted in a corner kick for The Bulls. Carey-Bertram and Jon Brady worked a quick, short corner and Carey-Bertram found space on the corner of the box to smash a shot across the face of the goal and into the far top corner, silencing the home fans and sending the travelling support or around 200 into delirium.

Aldershot were quick to remind United that they were still in the game and went close at the other end. Nick Crittenden soon forced Wayne Brown into a good save before Brady fired over at the other end following a cross from Ryan Green. Carey-Bertram then latched onto a through ball and was felled by Andre Boucaud, seemingly inside the penalty box, but the linesman indicated a foul right on the edge of the area. Another free kick, from Brady, fell to Bailey in the box but his shot was blocked and then Purdie had an even better opportunity but again a defender was in the way.

Four minutes before the break, Terry Brown made the first change of the game replacing Steve Watson with Ryan Scott. The Shots came out in the second half with renewed energy and had Hereford on the back foot for the most part of the second period. Blewitt was carded for a foul twenty five yards out, which required a good save by Brown to deny an equaliser. Stephen Reed put another set piece over the bar while, at the other end, Bailey shot at Nicki Bull when a corner found its way to him.

Scott Guyett saw a header clawed away by Brown as The Shots continued to pressure and then Tim Sills put a header wide. United almost finished the game, against the run of play, but Bull did well to tip the ball wide. With just over a hour gone, Brady managed to find Bailey in a good position and his shot on the turn appeared to be heading into the bottom corner but Bull saved well.

Perhaps the best chance for the hosts came when Crittenden's corner was touched on by Guyett and then nodded over, from two yards, by Chris McPhee. Although they had plenty of possession in attack, the United rear guard were very solid especially man of the match Mkandawire, who made several vital interventions.

United will be very happy that they managed to bounce back from the defeat at Halifax in what was quite a difficult game. There is no doubt that, now injuries are starting to clear up for The Shots, that it will not be long before they push up the table. The 4-4-2 formation seemed to breath new life into Hereford's side and certain players looked more comfortable with that system.

The atmosphere, as always, was excellent as both sets of supporters in the crowd of 2,656 sang all they way through the game.

HUFC: Brown, Green, Mkandawire, Blewitt, Jeannin, Purdie, Stanley, Ferrell, Brady, Bailey, Carey-Bertram. Subs: James, Mawson, Pitman, Williams, Evans.

ATFC: Bull, Hamilton, Heald, Guyett, Reed, Nick Crittenden, Watson, Boucaud, Deen, Sills, McPhee. Subs: Weait, Scott, Holloway, Barnard, Sulaimani.

Bulls fail at home again

Hereford United failed to use home advantage and go on to take all three points in another frustrating game at Edgar Street. The performance was not the worst, and perhaps United lacked the little bit of luck needed, but the result all the same will be very disappointing.

The Bulls didn't make a change to the side that started against Aldershot, but Dean Beckwith was named on the bench in place of Andy Williams, and the side, once again, started brightly. Alex Jeannin supplied the cross for Hereford's first chance, and young striker Matt Bailey, making his home debut, was on the end of it but his header was just wide at the far post, but he made amends with quarter of a hour gone.

Darren Blewitt cleared with his head and Danny Carey-Bertram's flick on was collected by Bailey who dinked the ball over the on rushing Richard McKinney in the Canvey Island goal to break the deadlock. However, the lead lasted just five minutes when The Gulls levelled with what was something of a freak goal. A corner was swung in from the right and Wayne Brown, who came to collect, fell in the box. The ball looped over him and was diverted into the back of the net by Alex Jeannin. The Hereford player's looked stunned, and turned towards referee Amy Rayner in appeal for a foul on their 'keeper.

Hereford lost the momentum that they had picked up previously and it took them a while to get back into their stride, and the game began to get scrappy with some questionable refereeing decisions. Patient build up led to a good cross from Rob Purdie on the left, and it was Dwaine Clarke who headed back

Hereford United v Canvey Island

Hereford United striker Graham Evans tries to find a way past Canvey defenders Chris Duffy and Ben Chenery.

Hereford United v Canvey Island.
GOAL... Matt Bailey fires Hereford into the lead against Canvey.

Hereford United v Canvey Island
Hereford United's Matt Bailey (2nd left) celebrates his goal against Canvey island with team mates as referee Amy Rayner looks on.

towards his own goal, forcing the 'keeper to back pedal in order to keep the ball out. Jason Hallet had a good chance to put the visitors in front when he was played through, put a low save from Brown denied him. Just before the break Craig Stanley came close to a second goal for United, but Bailey's head down, from Purdie's cross, was just ahead of him.

Rayner was again at the centre of things with three minutes gone in the second half, when Carey-Bertram worked space in the box and then appeared to have his legs taken away from him in the box, but Rayner waved the appeals away. Carey-Bertram then struck a snap shot just wide before Green found the run of Bailey in the box, but he was denied a shot on goal by a great last ditch challenge. Stanley was next to pick out the run of Bailey in behind the defence but this time the striker played a ball across the goal face, which Carey-Bertram couldn't quite stretch to.

Hallet was presented with a good chance out of nothing, when he found himself in acres of space in the box, but it seemed to surprise him and his tame shot was easy work for Brown. Tony James replaced the injured Blewitt soon after the hour mark and it was not long before Canvey were reduced to ten men, when Jeff Minton received his marching orders for a second yellow card, this time a late challenge on man of the match Carey-Bertram. Turner made a second change after this, bringing Graham Evans on for Jon Brady, and switching to three up front.

Carey-Bertram got himself ahead of the defence yet again, after shaking off the challenge of Dominic Sterling, but he missed the target from ten yards out. Sterling then had a good chance at the other end, but his shot after a free kick was saved by Brown. Green and Carey-Bertram both had shots before United thought they had secured the winner in the last minute.

Two corners in quick succession were won by the hosts and the second was headed back towards the near post by Bailey, where Jeannin came flying in and headed against the underside

Hereford United v Canvey Island.
Canvey Island 'keeper Richard McKinney punches clear under pressure from Hereford United's Tamika Mkandawire and Matt Bailey.

of the bar. The ball appeared to drop over the line but was quickly hooked away and Rayner decided, in another dubious decision, that it was not a goal and the game ended one goal apiece.

Once again United failed to go on and add to an early goal, and it has cost them dear. With most of the other results going their way, Hereford could well have made a good jump up the table. The draw means though, that they remain in seventh, when a win could have moved them up to fifth, just three points away from second place. The draw was very frustrating for the majority of the crowd of 2,500, which included 52 away fans.

HUFC: Brown, Green, Mkandawire, Blewitt, Jeannin, Purdie, Ferrell, Stanley, Brady, Bailey, Carey-Bertram. Subs: James, Beckwith, Mawson, Pitman, Evans.

CIFC: McKinney, Duffy, McGhee, Chenery, Sterling, Kennedy, Minton, Sedgemore, Clarke, Hallett, Ibe. Subs: Potter, Noto Gregory, Conroy, Tait.

Accrington Stanley v Hereford United, 7 October 2005. Report by Brian Goodwin

Brown Bullet kills off United

Another Hereford United old boy came back to haunt them last night as David Brown, who left for Accrington Stanley towards the end of last season, netted a fifty fifth minute winner to put his current side level on points at the top of the Conference.

Hereford's only change to the starting eleven was at the back where Tony James was recalled to the line up with Darren Blewitt making way. There was no place on the bench for Graham Evans and so Andy Williams took his place.

Within ten minutes of play, The Bulls already found themselves behind, although it was a controversial opener. Paul Mullin, who'd already been denied by Wayne Brown, collected the ball from a throw in and flicked it on for Ian Craney, who was one of two Accy players in an offside position, and he calmly slotted into the bottom corner. Hereford, who enjoyed large amounts of possession, failed to really trouble Darren Randolph until twenty minutes in, when a powerful free kick from Alex Jeannin was palmed behind for a corner.

Four minutes after, Andy Ferrell was given a golden opportunity to level things up, but after Randolph had denied Matt Bailey, he somehow managed to deny Ferrell who only had to force the ball over the line from no more than two yards. Hereford continued to have the better of things, but yet again didn't really trouble Randolph; Bailey came closest before the break with a header that went over the bar from a Jeannin corner.

United came out for the second half with renewed energy and pegged Accrington back within a minute of the restart. Craig Stanley dogged down Anthony Barry in the midfield, and played a perfect through ball for Danny Carey-Bertram who neatly slipped a shot beyond the reach of the 'keeper and into the far bottom corner. Hereford went onto enjoy their best spell of the game but the hosts replied against the run of play.

A corner, conceded by James when he blocked a shot, was flicked onto the far post where Brown was on hand to acrobatically smash the ball into the roof of the net for his sixth goal of the season. This was the last real threat that Accy really posed to the Hereford goal, but despite all the pressure from United, they couldn't find a second equaliser.

Man of the match Stanley tried to find some more passes to match his earlier one that assisted Carey-Bertram's goal, but with little success. With around twenty five minutes to go, Jeannin handed a perfect chance to Bailey with a cross whipped in from the left, but somehow the loanee failed, under no evident pressure from a marker, to connect with the goal gaping from little more than a yard out.

Frustration began to grow for Hereford, both on the pitch and on the terrace, not helped by the replacement of perhaps United's greatest threat Carey-Bertram, who seemed to pick up a hamstring injury. Andy Williams came on, and impressed and was perhaps unlucky not to do better with a couple of his efforts. Andy Ferrell was booked for dissent late on and Accrington held on to gain a valuable three points.

It has to be asked, how many more poor results can the pre-season favourites afford before the championship is out of their reach, even at this stage of the season. The increasingly worrying lack of goals needs to be resolved very quickly, and this perhaps will not be helped with the news that top scorer Carey-Bertram picked up an injury last night, although it is unknown how serious it is. The Bulls need to find some form very soon indeed, if they are to continue their promotion challenge, after yet another defeat in front of 1,603; the largest attendance at the Interlink Express Stadium this season.

HUFC: Brown, Green, Mkandawire, James, Jeannin, Purdie, Ferrell, Stanley, Brady, Bailey, Carey-Bertram. Subs: Blewitt, Beckwith, Mawson, Pitman, Williams.

ASFC: Randolph, Richardson, Flynn, Welch, Butler, Jagielka, Barry, Craney, Roberts, Mullin, Brown. Subs: Dibble, Cook, Ventre, Navarro, Mangan.

Hereford United v Burton Albion, 15 October 2005. Report by Brian Goodwin

James seals three points

Hereford United were 2-0 victors at Edgar Street this afternoon against a resistant Burton Albion side. United scored early and late on to defeat Albion, who have become a bit of a banana skin for Graham Turner's side in recent seasons. Turner started with the same side that lost against Accrington last weekend, with Matt Bailey and Danny Carey-Bertram recovering from knocks to take part.

Dale Anderson lasted for just ten minutes before he was replaced due to injury by Shaun Harrad. The first intent came from the visitors via Andy Todd, and he came even closer moments later with a shot that flew inches over Wayne Brown's crossbar. However, it was Hereford who made the break through with little more than twenty minutes gone.

Hereford United v Burton Albion
Hereford United's Tamika Mkandawire beats Burton Albion skipper Darren Stride in an aerial duel.

Tamika Mkandawire played a long ball out of the defence, which was edged on by Bailey for his strike partner. Carey-Bertram raced, and beat, 'keeper Saul Deeney to the ball and lobbed over the advancing 'keeper, before getting clattered by him for his fourth goal in five games. Hereford played out the half in good form, and could have gone further in front. Craig Stanley's half volley was well tipped over from twenty yards before Mkandawire saw a header hooked off the line.

Hereford United v Burton Albion
Hereford captain Tony James celebrates scoring United's second in front of the Meadow End with team mate Jon Brady. Not looking so happy is Burton goalkeeper Saul Deeney.

Stanley had another good chance when he, surprisingly, found himself with a clear view of goal but his low shot was gathered by Deeney. In a rare Burton attack Jon Shaw got in behind the defence but Alex Jeannin was back to make an important block while, at the other end, Andy Ferrell shot just wide when Bailey touched down for him. Albion made a second sub before the break, again due to injury, with Andy Todd being replaced by Andy Ducros.

Man of the match Mkandawire almost doubled Hereford's lead moments after the restart, but he somehow directed his header, from Jeannin's corner, wide from inside the six yard box. Burton began to put some pressure on The Bulls and had a few efforts on goal, but nothing that Brown couldn't deal with. Perhaps the most nervy moment was when

Hereford United v Burton Albion

PENALTY... Burton Albion skipper Darren Stride holds back Hereford striker Andy Williams. Referee Mr Langford awarded the decision to Hereford and Stride was sent off!!

Mkandawire gifted the ball to Ducros just inside the half, and he went to chip Brown, but the 'keeper back pedalled to make what was in the end an easy catch.

Stanley again threatened but this time his thunderous shot smashed against a defender while Shaw headed wide for the visitors. Stanley was then, strangely, replaced by Jamie Pitman when it seemed that he was having a good game. Brown had to be on his toes to deny Terry Henshaw, whose shot was heading for the top corner. Albion did manage to get the ball in the net but it was ruled offside.

Hereford United v Burton Albion.
Hereford skipper Tony James challenges Burton Albion's Andy Corbett for a header.

Turner then made a second change, and once again it seemed to be the wrong person who was replaced. Carey-Bertram, rather than Bailey, made way for Andy Williams, who seemed to spur United into life and it was the youngster who won the decisive penalty. He took control of Jon Brady's ball into the middle before being upended by Darren Stride, who received his marching orders having picked up two yellow cards. Tony James stepped up to fire into the bottom corner in front of the Meadow End, sending Deeney the wrong way and wrapping up the victory.

Despite emerging comfortable winners, and scoring more than once for the first time since the away win at Crawley, United still did not impress most of the 2,493 spectators, including 155 Burton fans. The fluent passing that Hereford have become customised with still appears to be missing this season and it is making the team boring to watch. The three points are what matter though, and United move up one place but are eight points off the top.

HUFC: Brown, Green, Mkandawire, James, Jeannin, Purdie, Ferrell, Stanley, Brady, Bailey, Carey-Bertram. Subs: Blewitt, Beckwith, Mawson, Pitman, Williams.

BAFC: Deeney, Corbett, Tinson, Austin, Webster, Hall, Bell, Stride, Todd, Anderson, Shaw. Subs: Harrad, Graves, Ducros, Crane, Henshaw.

Mansfield Town v Hereford United, 18 October 2005. Report by Brian Goodwin

Stags bow out at hands of Bulls

Hereford United put in a solid away performance to knock a Mansfield side, who are currently rock bottom of the Football League, out of the LDV Vans Trophy Northern Section first round. Hereford's side saw many changes from the one that defeated Burton last Saturday, which saw the inclusion of Guy Ipoua although only as a substitute. Craig Mawson was named in goal and there were also places for Jamie Pitman and Andy Williams, who both came on as subs against Burton.

Adrian Littlejohn had the first sniff of goal when he capitalised on a slip by Tony James but he shot early, and his effort was wide. The first real attack on the Stags' goal was after twelve minutes, and it was then when United took the lead. A good move found Jon Brady in possession on the right and his cross was controlled by Rob Purdie whose shot was parried away by the 'keeper. The ball fell to Rhys Day in the six yard box but his clearance was denied by Matt Bailey, who then simply poked the ball home from inside the box.

The Stags replied well but still Mawson didn't have much to deal with. Adam Birchall's shot was off target while Bailey had another good chance for The Bulls, but he sliced Brady's cross onto the roof of the net. Mansfield could have been level before the break though, when a loose ball found its way in behind the Hereford defence where Adrian Littlejohn was waiting, but Mawson was quickly off his line to make a good stop.

The hosts came out with seemingly renewed confidence for the second half and had a good spell of pressure, where they had Hereford camped inside their own half. Alex Jeannin had to get back quickly to make a recovering block as Jake Buxton threatened before Gavin Peers saw a long range effort palmed around the post by Mawson. Andy Ferrell and Jeannin both had efforts on goal, but neither really troubled Jason White. Pitman, who teamed up well with man of the match Ferrell in the middle, created two great chances within minutes of each other as The Whites pushed for a second goal. His through ball firstly set away Williams who was denied when one on one with White and then Purdie was to benefit from another defence splitting pass but his low drive was palmed away.

With fifteen minutes left, Graham Turner introduced Ipoua in the place of Bailey and ten minutes after Graham Evans followed, in place of Williams. James headed wide from a Purdie cross and late on Ipoua hit the side netting with a powerful effort from a narrow angle, when perhaps it would have been better to centre.

United should be very pleased with the performance as they managed to rest a couple of first team players and still progress to the second round against League opposition. Something of concern maybe that Ryan Green, Ferrell, Pitman and Brady were all booked during the course of the game and will all be an extra card closer to a suspension. The 90 away supporters, in a crowd of 1,393, sang all the way through what was a reasonably entertaining game, in a very decent all-seater stadium, unlike the home fans who made less noise than you'd hear in a library!

HUFC: Mawson, Green, James, Mkandawire, Jeannin, Purdie, Ferrell, Pitman, Brady, Williams, Bailey. Subs: Beckwith, Stanley, Lewis, Evans, Ipoua.

MTFC: White, Jacobs, Talbot, Day, Baptiste, Lloyd, McLachlan, Dawson, Arnold, Birchall, Littlejohn. Subs: Jelleyman , Buxton, Peers, Heron, Coke.

Hereford United v Alfreton Town, 22 October 2005. Report by Brian Goodwin

Firepower lacking once again

Hereford United were once again short of the creative spark that they have been lacking so often this season as Alfreton Town pulled off one of the shocks of the fourth qualifying round at Edgar Street this afternoon. The goalless draw means that the two teams meet again this Tuesday night as they fight it out for a place in the first round proper of the FA Cup, against Cambridge City.

Just one change was made to the side that defeated Mansfield in the week; Danny Carey-Bertram was recalled to the starting line up so Andy Williams dropped to the bench. There was no place for the injured Darren Blewitt and Craig Mawson kept his place in goal as Wayne Brown has been told by Chester that he cannot play in any Cup games during his loan spell at Edgar Street.

Hereford United v Alfreton Town FA Cup.
Hereford midfielder Jamie Pitman heads clear an Alfreton cross.

Hereford United v Alfreton Town FA Cup.
Hereford midfielder Andy Ferrell gets to grips with Alfreton's David Robinson.

Hereford United v Alfreton Town FA Cup.
FLYING TACKLE... Hereford forward Daniel Carey-Bertram and Alfreton Town defender Mark Turner. Mark Turner is the son of Hereford manager Graham.

The first half saw a series of half chances for the hosts, but they did not really trouble the Alfreton goalkeeper. Jon Brady had picked out Carey-Bertram on the flank and his cross was cut out at the last moment as it headed towards Matt Bailey before Bailey failed to connect with a Andy Ferrell effort, following some good build up play involving Carey-Bertram. A pot shot from thirty yards almost caught Mawson out for the visitors, but the ball flashed into the side netting before United broke via Rob Purdie and then Carey-Bertram, who hit the side netting himself.

The best chance of the half was then to arrive, when Brady whipped in a corner from the right, Tamika Mkandawire stole in front of his marker but his glancing header fell inches wide of the upright. Jon Stevenson, ever dangerous for Town, was gifted the ball by Alex Jeannin, just before the break, but his run and bouncing shot was claimed at the second attempt by Mawson.

Purdie was denied by a brilliant tip over the bar soon after the restart, having been played in by Ferrell but it was Stevenson who should have broken the deadlock with fifty minutes on the clock. Tony James miss controlled a long ball forward, allowing Stevenson a clear run on goal, but his drive flew across the goal face.

Mkandawire again went close with a header, this time seeing it go just over, when Purdie returned an over hit corner from Brady into the box. Bailey had two good efforts, but neither of which were too much trouble for Legzoins. Purdie again linked up well with Carey-Bertram, but this time it was Ferrell's shot that missed the target. Graham Turner then made two changes to try and freshen things up and get his side out of a whole. Guy Ipoua and Andy Williams both came on to form an all changed strike force.

The change almost worked with seven minutes remaining; Jeannin's cross was met by Williams' diving header, but he was denied by a great save. Pitman was first to the loose ball and centred the ball to Ipoua who, from around four yards, somehow managed to lift the ball over the bar when it seemed impossible to miss. His shot was the last threat of what was a very poor second half

Hereford United v Alfreton Town FA Cup.
Hereford's Tamika Mkandawire, Matt Bailey and Tony James rue a missed chance.

but there was still time for Jeannin to pick up his fifth booking of the season, this one for dissent, meaning that he misses the upcoming replay.

The crowd was also very low for Edgar Street; it would appear that the attendances are beginning to resemble the performances being put in by Hereford. It was the lowest of the season at Edgar Street and it was aided by the noisy 97 Alfreton fans, in a crowd of 1,768.

HUFC: Mawson, Green, James, Mkandawire, Jeannin, Purdie, Ferrell, Pitman, Brady, Bailey, Carey Bertram. Subs: Beckwith, Stanley, Evans, Ipoua, Williams.

ATFC: Alfreton Town: Legzoins, Clarke, Featherstone, Blount, Turner, David Robinson, Blunt, Fisher, Godber, Stevenson, Mills Subs: Ross, Duffield, Woolley, Nwadike, Powell

Alfreton Town v Hereford United (Replay), 25 October 2005. Report by Brian Goodwin

Poor Bulls scrape through

It needed a replay, extra time and then a penalty shoot out for Hereford United to finally dispose of their lower league opposition Alfreton Town in the F.A. Cup Fourth Qualifying round but following the 1-1 draw last night, The Bulls find themselves in the first round proper with an away tie at Cambridge City. Ryan Green was missing for the Bulls and so Rob Purdie filled in at right back, making way for Craig Stanley to come back into the midfield, in United's only squad change from the side that started on Saturday.

Although the home side started well at the Impact Arena, it was Hereford who posed the first threats at goal. Early on Jon Brady had the away supporters thinking his twenty yard effort was flying into the bottom corner, but it drifted inches wide. Brady turned supplier for United's next shot; his free kick fell in the box to Tamika Mkandawire, whose shot on the turn was palmed behind by Adam Legzdins. Stanley shot wide for Hereford again before Jon Stevenson linked up with Gary Mills but his effort was just wide.

The Bulls should have taken the lead just before the half hour mark, but the cross bar denied Mkandawire from close range and with little more than half an hour gone, it was the hosts who fired in front. A half cleared corner fell to Jason Blunt on the left and his cross was met by a flying header which beat Craig Mawson at his near post, and to add insult to injury for Graham Turner, it was his son, Mark, who'd netted. Alfreton played out the half the much better side as the travelling fans' frustration grew.

The second half began much the same but then, on fifty three minutes, Craig Stanley popped up with an unlikely equaliser, with his head! Man of the match Jon Brady, a constant threat down the right, cracked in another great cross and Stanley was on the end of it at the far post, leaving the 'keeper with no chance. Alfreton lost a key player, Chris Bettney, through injury and picked up a couple of bookings and they appeared rattled by the goal. Danny Carey-Bertram fired over in his last contribution, as Andy Williams was introduced up front with ten minutes of the half remaining.

Andy Ferrell intercepted a ball across the defence with five minutes to go and raced clear, before squaring to Williams who, from six yards, failed to convert as Legzdins made himself big and turned the ball behind. Then, in the final moments, a golden chance fell to Godder, but having beaten Purdie to a cross, somehow directed his header wide of the mark and thus, the game went into extra time.

The first half of the added period saw the introduction of Guy Ipoua with the largely ineffective Matt Bailey making way. The extra time saw one good chance either side of half time for United; in the first Alex Jeannin smashed a left footed drive across the goal face and wide and after the break, Purdie was played in, running in from the right, but his powerful drive was parried away. The result remained at 1-1 after 120 minutes of football meaning a penalty shoot out would decide the tie.

Tony James stepped up confidently and hammered in Hereford's first, to level things up but Ferrell saw his shot brilliantly saved meaning it was still 1-1 after two penalties each. Williams and Graham Evans, who came on for the injured Stanley late on in extra time, both saw their penalties go in, although the 'keeper got a hand to both as Craig Mawson saved a second penalty leaving it up to Guy Ipoua to win the match with United's final penalty. The experienced Cameroonian made no mistake either as he smashed the ball down the middle of the goal, much to the relief of the travelling 150 or so fans in a crowd of 740.

HUFC: Mawson, Purdie, James, Mkandawire, Jeannin, Ferrell, Pitman, Stanley, Brady, Bailey, Carey-Bertram. Subs: Beckwith, Blewitt, Evans, Williams, Ipoua.

ATFC: A Legzdins, R Clarke, L Featherstone, M Blount, M Turner, D Robinson, J Blunt, M Fisher, M Godber, J Stevenson, C Bettney. Subs: N Ross, L Powell, C White, P Duffield, E Nwadike.

Derby day ends in draw

The much anticipated meeting of Hereford United and Kidderminster Harriers at Aggborough finished in a 1-1 draw this afternoon but it will be the hosts who will perhaps feel most aggrieved that they did not collect all three points. At the start of the afternoon, many felt that a draw would be a good result for The Harriers but when they levelled things up with just under half an hour gone, they didn't look back.

Hereford United put out a make-shift back four as injuries and suspensions took their toll, leaving Graham Turner with no full backs to choose from. Rob Purdie and Darren Blewitt took the positions up and helped in what was a good defensive showing.

The travelling army of Bulls fan's were sent into raptures with no more than six minutes gone, when Jamie Pitman broke the deadlock. He found himself with a clear run at goal twenty five yards out, but hesitated and a recovering tackle sent the ball air bound. However, it bounced perfectly and Pitman hit a spectacular volley into the roof of the net. The Bulls pushed on from then and created a couple of chances. Firstly Danny Carey-Bertram was just inches from connecting with Andy Ferrell's back post cross and then Jon Brady fired over.

However, with twenty eight minutes gone, Harriers broke against the run of play and netted an equaliser. Simon Russell delivered a pin-point cross for Taiwo Atieno to head in from close range. Tamika Mkandawire had to be on his toes to put in a good challenge as Russell forced his way towards goal and the centre back was busy at the other end moments later. Brady swung in a cross and

Kidderminster Harriers v Hereford United

Hereford United defender Tamika Mkandawire outjumps team mate Jamie Pitman and Kidderminster's Taiwo Atieno.

Kidderminster Harriers v Hereford United

Hereford's Andy Ferrell chased by a Kidderminster player.

Kidderminster Harriers v Hereford United
Kidderminster's Simon Russell takes a shot watched by Hereford's Rob Purdie and Jamie Pitman.

Mkandawire rose above everyone to smash a header into the back of the net, but referee Bob Desmond gave a free kick the other way.

United continued their search for a second goal and man of the match Pitman, who popped up anywhere where a tackle was needed for the visitors, almost struck glory once again. He unleashed an unstoppable shot that was destined for the top corner, until taking the slightest of deflections off the back of Matt Bailey. On the stroke of half time Brady again switched play to Ferrell, who this time picked out Carey-Bertram, put his volley went across the goal face.

Bailey was replaced at the break, giving youngster Andy Williams a chance to shine, and although he didn't score, he posed a threat in the United attack. Atieno was again causing problems for United's defence with his height and power and moments after the restart skinned Tony James, only to be denied by a super block by Craig Stanley. Mkandawire again caused problems from a corner, but this time nodded over and he was then on defensive duties to hook away a dangerous effort from Russell. With fifteen minutes left, Guy Ipoua was introduced and Carey-Bertram made way.

Harriers began to mount some pressure on Hereford in the final stages and pretty much had United boxed in their own half, expect from some counter attacking football by The Whites. Wayne Brown reacted brilliantly to deny what seemed a certain goal from Atieno; he met a quick-fire cross with his head and Brown somehow tipped over from point blank range. Brown then did well to

Kidderminster Harriers v Hereford United

Hereford United goalscorer Jamie Pitman celebrates scoring with team mates Andy Ferrell, Darren Blewitt and Craig Stanley.

punch away a header from the resulting corner to keep the scores even.

United were soon on the break with Andy Williams, who beat his man on the edge of the box but was then forced wide and could only win a corner off the 'keeper, Dan Lewis. Ipoua then created a good chance for substitute Dean Beckwith, who'd replaced the injured Blewitt, and the defender saw his low effort deflected just inches wide, as the 'keeper had been wrong footed. A final chance for Harriers in injury time fell to Russell in the middle, but his effort was blocked by an on-rushing yellow shirt.

It turned out to be quite an entertaining game for the neutral supporter, but for the Hereford fans, of which their was at least 1,000 (later confirmed as 1031) in a crowd of 3,241, it was a disappointing result in a game, before hand, many expected to win. The lack of an attacking force was once again evident for The Bulls who must be craving the return to fitness of several key players, including Adam Stansfield and Ipoua in attack.

HUFC: Brown, Purdie, Mkandawire, James, Blewitt, Ferrell, Pitman, Stanley, Brady, Bailey, Carey-Bertram. Subs: Beckwith, Mawson, Williams, Evans, Ipoua.

KHFC: Lewis, Mullins, Burgess, Hatswell, Jackson, O'Connor, Fleming, Sheldon, Russell, Atieno, Heslop. Subs: Thompson, Danby, Burton, Hurren, Wilson.

Cambridge City v Hereford United, 4 November 2005. Report by Kevin Goodwin

Bulls scrape into second round

Hereford United reached Round Two of the FA Cup for a second successive season thanks to a strike from Jon Brady. He struck with 12 minutes left on the clock sending the Bulls into the hat for the draw on Sunday. Hereford are ball number 22.

Graham Turner made changes from the side that drew at Aggborough last weekend, with striker Guy Ipoua returning to the first side, Andy Williams also started with Danny Carey-Bertram dropping to the bench, and Matt Bailey returning to Crewe. Andy Ferrell dropped to the bench with Rob Purdie returning to his normal left side role, Ryan Green returned at right back. Alex Jeannin also returned after suspension, replacing Darren Blewitt who picked up a knock at Kidderminster last Saturday. Craig Mawson also returned to the side, as Wayne Brown is ineligible to play any Cup competition. Darren Knurek, signed from Evensham as a back up goalkeeper for the FA Cup was on the bench.

United had the better of the opening stages, Jeannin's pass was collected by Brady who let fly a low shot from 25 yards but Cambridge City 'keeper Naisbitt was on hand to hold the shot. Williams turned well before firing a left footed shot over the bar. Hereford's best chance of a lacklustre first half fell to Tamika Mkandawire, he leapt well to meet a corner from Brady, but his header was cleared off the line by the defender, although it looked as though it was heading just wide.

Cambridge came back into it towards the end of the first half and Dale Binns found space on the left hand side of the box but he fired his shot wide of Mawson's goal. Ipoua held the ball up well, and he set up Jamie Pitman who failed to get his shot away, the defender made a superb challenge but the ball came off Pitman's foot and went wide. Cambridge thought they had taken the lead just minutes before half time when Mark Molesley had been played through, he rounded Mawson and fired into an empty net only for his celebrations to be short lived, the linesman giving offside. The last action of the first half fell to Robbie Simpson who fired just over with a volley.

Like the first half, Hereford started the second half better and were creating more chances than Cambridge City. Alex Jeannin won a free kick down the left, and he fired in a cross to Ipoua, who managed to get in an overhead kick despite having his shirt held, but the shot didn't trouble the 'keeper and went over. Despite a lot of possession, Hereford failed to make it count until Purdie managed to find a yard and shoot, but the defender deflected the ball over.

Williams was quiet but could have given Hereford the lead when his smart turn found him space on the edge of the area but his low shot was just wide of Naisbitt's goal. Pitman then tried to make it two goals out of two games, when he fired in a long range drive, but it didn't trouble the 'keeper. Graham Evans then got a run out replacing youngster Williams.

Cambridge City once again came back into it towards the latter stages of the half, Brady giving away a free kick, the ball was swept in, but the clearance by Hereford found Green. He ran the length of the pitch beating two players on his way before passing left footed to Brady whose explosive shot, with the outside of his right foot, curled into the back of the net giving the 'keeper absolutely no chance of saving it.

City made some late changes in search of an equaliser with Michael Gash replacing Craig Dobson and Jamie Southon coming on for Josh Simpson. And it was the substitute Gash who tested Mawson with little left on the clock. Craig Pope laid-off to him but Gash's powerful shot was straight at the Hereford goalie.

It was a slightly disappointing game played by both sides, on a relatively good pitch. Hereford were looking for Ipoua at nearly every occasion, with Ipoua not winning much in the air and looking better on the ground when the ball was played to his feet. The defence was once again solid and another clean sheet is a bonus. The game was watched by 1,116 fans with 191 making the long trip from Hereford. The away fans went home happier, despite an average performance, and are through to the next round.

HUFC: Mawson, Green, Jeannin, Mkandawire, James, Brady, Pitman, Stanley, Purdie, Ipoua, Williams. Subs: Knurek, Carey-Bertram, Evans, Ferrell, Beckwith.

Cambridge City: Naisbitt, Pope, Chaffey, Fuff, Langston, Dobson, Josh Simpson, Molesley, Binns, Robbie Simpson, Booth. Subs: Calton, Wilson, Smith, Gash, Southon.

Hereford United v Woking, 12 November 2005. Report by Brian Goodwin

Bulls are ace against The Cards

Hereford United manager Graham Turner was granted his pre-match wish of "more goals" from his side as United swept aside a Woking side who were level on points with their opponents and on a twelve game unbeaten run prior to the game. However, the

Hereford United v Woking.
Hereford forward Guy Ipoua scores in the 4-0 defeat of Woking.

run came to an abrupt end as the hosts put in their best overall performance of the season in an entertaining encounter.

United, who were unchanged from last Friday, threatened first before Justin Richards, who'd netted ten times this league campaign, has two efforts off target. Guy Ipoua almost put his side in front early on when he found himself one on one inside the box, but his effort was denied by Shwan Jalal in the Woking goal. The Cameroonian then turned provider as Hereford took the lead on the half hour mark. He mugged a defender of the ball in the corner before finding Andy Williams who finished with a low drive beyond the reach of Jalal.

Hereford United v Woking.
Hereford forward Andy Williams celebrates scoring against Woking.

This obviously worked wonders for both Williams' and Herefords' confidence and Jon Brady almost doubled the lead with a cracking half volley from twenty-five yards, but it was deflected over. Craig Mawson had to be alert at the other end as he firstly fumbled a cross from the right, but then redeemed himself by putting in a vital tackle on the ground as several attackers lurked. In first half injury time United almost scored a second, but Ipoua, who was offside anyway, headed straight at Jalal when he really should have converted.

The second half was all one way traffic and the result could well have been really embarrassing for the Cards if it wasn't for some good goalkeeping. Tamika Mkandawire paced out of defence before finding the run of Williams minutes after the restart, and Mkandawire was first to the rebounded shot of Williams, but somehow lifted the ball over a gaping net. Ipoua then made an opening for Williams, who saw his shot saved, before he was involved in United's second goal.

Ipoua did excellently to hold off a challenge before releasing Brady on the right, and his far post cross was met by Rob Purdie who managed to slide the ball in for 2-0. It was then Woking who attacked, a rare thing in the

Hereford United v Woking.
Hereford United 'keeper Craig Mawson punches clear in the game against Woking watched by captain Tony James and defender Alex Jeannin.

Hereford United v Woking.
Hereford United's Graham Evans is just beaten to a cross by the Woking goalkeeper Shwan Jalal.

second period, but after a nice ball inside Alex Jeannin, Richards saw his shot turned behind for a corner. Brady was soon replaced as he took a knock, Danny Carey-Bertram taking his place on the right, and it was just five minutes later when United went further in front.

Rob Purdie received a return ball from Williams, and continued his run into the penalty area before firing a great shot into the far top corner from around twelve yards. And if that wasn't enough in the way of goals for Turner, Ipoua completed the rout just two minutes later. Jeannin was the provider this time, with a perfect through ball and Ipoua unleashed an unstoppable shot in to the back of the net, via the cross bar. It was his last action of the match, that capped a man of the match performance, as Graham Evans took his place. Soon after, Andy Ferrell took Williams' place as United continued their attacking intentions.

Lloyd Blackman had fired just wide for The Cards, but both Ferrell and Evans could have added to the score line in the last ten minutes. Carey-Bertram had cut back to Evans, but his shot was decent enough, just Jalal was equal for it and then Evans provided a cross for Ferrell but his effort was deflected over the bar.

The performance was the best, overall, of the season and Turner will be delighted with the goals scored, but will be equally pleased that The Bulls have maintained their impressive defensive record, aided by some brilliant performances by Tony James and Mkandawire. The creative spark of Ipoua, who had a hand in two of the goals and got one for himself, though was enough to clinch him the man of the match award. Hereford will be desperate to maintain this form as they intend to push up the Conference table.

HUFC: Mawson, Green, James, Mkandawire, Jeannin, Purdie, Pitman, Stanley, Brady, Williams, Ipoua. Subs: Beckwith, Brown, Ferrell, Evans, Carey-Bertram.

WFC: Jalal, Jackson, Nethercott, Oliver, El-Salahi, Ferguson, Murray, Smith, Evans, McAllister, Richards. Subs: Davies, Cockerill, Rawle, Selley, Blackman.

United finally string two together

Hereford United followed up last weeks impressive victory against Woking with a solid away victory at the Glynn Hopkin Stadium, as Dagenham & Redbridge hosted The Bulls. Graham Turner was able to name an unchanged starting eleven, but Karl Lewis was promoted to the subs bench to cover for the injured Wayne Brown.

Hereford, who had previously beaten The Daggers just once in the Conference, started the game in brilliant fashion, carrying on from where they left off against Woking. Guy Ipoua had headed wide at the far post when play had been well switched to the right and Andy Williams had fired wide before United took a twelfth minute lead.

Ryan Green again linked up well with Jon Brady on the right to deliver a cross for Ipoua, whose header was palmed into the path of Williams by Tony Roberts in the home goal. Williams somehow planted the ball against the post, from a yard out with the goal gaping, before he was able to tap the ball in from the rebound; a huge relief to the youngster as he saved himself the embarrassment of an awful miss.

Four minutes later the young attacker headed on target again, from a Brady cross, but Roberts claimed the ball this time and with twenty five minutes gone Rob Purdie should have doubled the advantage. He played a neat one-two with Williams, but when he had a god sight on goal he tamely shot straight down the throat of the 'keeper.

United continued their attractive attacking football throughout the half and Brady should have done better at the far post, but sliced over, and should have had the game wrapped up by half time but it was the home side who almost pulled level, in injury time. Luckily a Paul Benson free header at the far post was blocked by Craig Mawson.

The second half was basically dominated by Dagenham, in terms of possession at least, and United seemed to have lost that spark that they showed all the way through the opening half. However, a counter attack led by Purdie on the left should have resulted in Hereford's second, but Jamie Pitman, a contender for man of the match with Tamika Mkandawire, was denied by the inside of the post having seen his shot beat the on rushing Roberts. The Daggers still failed to convert their possession into chances and it was United, again on the break, who threatened next via Craig Stanleys' header but it was easy for Roberts.

With fifteen minutes remaining The Bulls replaced Williams with Danny Carey-Bertram, but he had little affect on the game as service was limited from the midfield. Purdie hit a low snap shot forcing Roberts into another save and with six minutes left on the clock Turner took the decision to replace Brady with another defender, Dean Beckwith. The decision paid off as Beckwith's height was helpful in the closing stages that saw a fair few crosses whipped into United's box, but again there was nothing to trouble Mawson, who made a rare save in the final moments, pushing Mackail-Smith's shot around the post.

The result is just what United needed following their victory against Woking, and it is the first time this campaign that they have managed to string two league victories together. The two hundred or so away supporters in a crowd of 1,294 were entertained and would have been delighted with the first half of football produced by their side, but the second half was no where near the standard shown in the previous 135 minutes of football played by United.

HUFC: Mawson, Green, James, Mkandawire, Jeannin, Purdie, Pitman, Stanley, Brady, Williams, Ipoua. Subs: Beckwith, Ferrell, Lewis, Evans, Carey-Bertram.

D&RFC: Roberts, Foster, Blackett, Uddin, Griffiths, Goodwin, Southam, Bruce, Moore, Mackail-Smith, Benson. Subs: Cole Overland, Frota, Ward, Kenny Clark.

Hereford United v Port Vale, 22 November 2005. Report by Brian Goodwin

Bulls dump out second league side

Hereford United, having disposed of Mansfield Town in the first round, knocked out a second league side in the second round of the LDV Vans Trophy Northern Section at Edgar Street this evening. Injury struck League One outfit Port Vale were the opponents and the Bulls overcame them after extra time.

Two changes were made from the side that beat Dagenham; Andy Williams and Tony James were rested meaning recalls to the side for Danny Carey-Bertram and Dean Beckwith, who performed well at the back alongside stand in skipper Tamika Mkandawire. Guy Ipoua showed the first goal scoring intentions but sliced wide early on and then, following some great link up play, Jamie Pitman fired over from outside of the box.

United, who'd started the better, took the lead with fourteen minutes on the clock, when a free kick move paid off. Pitman had laid the ball onto Jon Brady whose shot was turned into the air off a defender, and Carey-Bertram watched the ball closely and volleyed into the back of the net, via the post, from ten yards out. Vale, who were pretty poor for a League One side, got back into the game and dominated the rest of the half, but United's defence reduced them to just a few long

Hereford United v Port Vale LDV Vans Trophy.
Goal… Hereford's Daniel Carey-Bertram scores the first against Port Vale.

Hereford United v Port Vale LDV Vans Trophy.
GOAL... Hereford's Tamika Mkandawire heads the winner against Port Vale.

range efforts. Chris Cornes and Andy Porter shot wide, while in between a free kick from Tony Dinning was blocked by Craig Mawson and cleared behind by Mkandawire.

The first chance from close range for Vale fell in the single added minute at the end of the first half, and it resulted in the equaliser. Jeff Smith was on the end of Cornes cross, and headed into the bottom corner unchallenged having lost his marker.

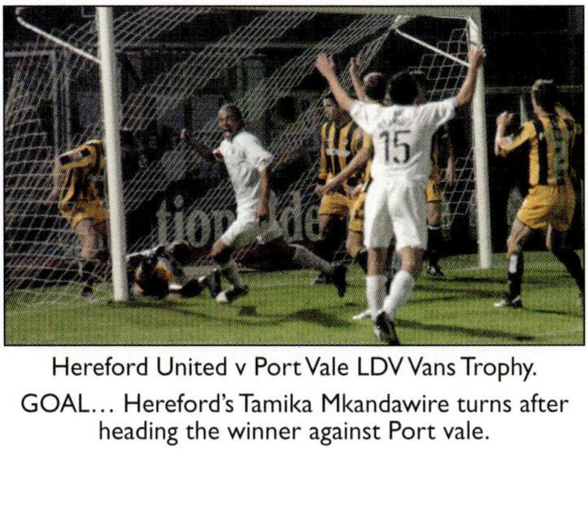

Hereford United v Port Vale LDV Vans Trophy.
GOAL... Hereford's Tamika Mkandawire turns after heading the winner against Port vale.

Nathan Lowndes hit the side netting in the opening stages of the second half with a cheeky back heel but United began to get a foot hold on the game once again. Graham Evans was introduced in place of Ipoua ten minutes into the half and he had a good chance when Pitman slipped Brady's cross into him, but the eccentric Johnathan Brain denied him. Lowndes should have put the visitors in front, but somehow managed to head a corner over, from pretty much under the cross bar and then, soon after Adam Stansfield had replaced Pitman, Robin Hulbert shot wide.

Stansfield had a good effort from twenty yards, that crept just wide of the far post and Simon Travis' appearance late on for Ryan Green was the last of the action for the ninety minutes. Extra time began with Brady giving the travelling 152 Vale fans a scare, when his intended cross clipped the cross bar and went over. Cornes volleyed over in front of the meadow end, before Mkandawire capped a man of the match performance with a goal, much to the delight of the majority of the crowd of 1,355. He met Alex Jeannin's corner with a downward header that avoided several defenders in the box and crept into the back of the net. United were able to play out the three remaining minutes of the first period and the whole of the second period by keeping the ball and frustrating their league opposition.

Much like the game at Dagenham on Saturday, The Bulls started well although they seemingly faded in the second half but were never really troubled by Port Vale. However, they will be delighted with result that sees them in the hat for the third round northern section, to be drawn next Saturday morning.

HUFC: Mawson, Green, Beckwith, Mkandawire, Jeannin, Purdie, Pitman, Stanley, Brady, Carey-Bertram, Ipoua. Subs: Travis, Lewis, Stansfield, Ferrell, Evans.

PVFC: Brain, Togwell, Pilkington, Dinning, James, Cornes, Innes, Sonner, Smith, Lowndes, Mulligan. Subs: Goodlad, Porter, Husbands, Rowland, Cardle.

Hereford United v Port Vale LDV Vans Trophy. Hereford manager Graham Turner shouts orders from the dugout with assistant manager John Trewick watching the game.

Hereford United v Exeter City, 26 November 2005. Report by Brian Goodwin

Exeter excel in ten minute spell

Hereford United hosted high-flyers Exeter City at Edgar Street this afternoon and will be most disappointed with the result, having completely dominated the first half. Three changes were made to the Hereford side with Andy Williams and Tony James returning and Simon Travis deputising for Ryan Green, who failed a late fitness test on an ankle injury sustained against Port Vale.

United started brilliantly and almost immediately opened the scoring when Craig Stanley received a pass to the left of the goal, but he centred the ball to Andy Williams, whose shot was blocked, when perhaps he would have been better off shooting himself. Moments later another good passing move found Jamie Pitman in the box. He crossed for Guy Ipoua and his downward header from six yards was brilliantly palmed behind by Paul Jones.

Stanley again came close to breaking the deadlock, this time with a wonderful thirty yard effort. He met a loose ball with a swing of the right boot and the curling effort had beaten Jones, who was off his line, but hit the underside of the cross bar before bouncing, off the line according to the officials, away to safety. Pitman set Rob Purdie racing away on the left with an awesome cross field pass, and Purdie beat his man before firing over from outside of the box. Purdie had a better chance of the stroke of half time, but he couldn't fully connect with Ipoua's cross and Jones made the save, to end a half dominated by the hosts, in which Exeter had only one shot.

The second period was a much different affair as Exeter came out and took the game to The Bulls. Les Afful was soon to be replaced by Steve Flack and it would seem that this change did a lot to help The Grecians as they started a spell of ten minutes in which they had United camped in their own half. Flack provided a through ball to Farrell who was only denied by a Tony James block but then disaster struck for United's skipper.

Hereford thought they should have won a free kick for hand ball on the edge of the City box, but it was not given and Exeter broke away. James intercepted a pass and seemingly under no pressure, slipped a ball back towards Craig Mawson. However, Jamie Mackie raced onto the lax pass and rounded the hesitant Mawson before sliding the ball into the back of the net.

Exeter continued to press as Hereford fell to bits and almost doubled the lead a minute later. Mawson did well to tip away a shot from inside the box and then a header at the far post was somehow turned over the bar by

Hereford United v Exter City
Hereford's Alex Jeannin blocks Exeter City's Les Afful.

Exeter old boy Alex Jeannin. The corner almost flew into the back of the net, via a Exeter head, but Jon Brady managed to get it away however the pressure paid off two minutes later when The Grecians made it 2-0.

Jon Challinor had worked himself some space in the box, received a through ball, and was given far to much time twelve yards out as he looked up, picked his spot, and planted the ball right in the far top corner sending the

Hereford United v Exter City
John Challinor's shot beats Hereford 'keeper Craig Mawson to make it 0-2.

Hereford United v Exter City

Exeter City players remonstrate with the referee after their captain Glenn Cronin fouled Guy Ipoua. Cronin was booked for the challenge.

Hereford United v Exter City

Exeter City's Chris Todd beats Hereford's Guy Ipoua with the help of team mate Danny Woodards.

790 away fans into raptures. United had needed to make a change after the first goal, as it was obvious that Exeter were getting a foothold on the game and heads had dropped after conceding. However, it was too late when Danny Carey-Bertram was introduced in the place of Jon Brady. The only response United could find was following a cross field pass from Jeannin, and Carey-Bertram'' delivery being headed narrowly over by Ipoua.

United, in front of their biggest crowd of the season (3,754), failed to make their chances count and paid the heavy price in the end. It has to be said that they made Exeter seem extremely ordinary in the first half but The Grecians' persistence paid off and a second half spell made all the difference in the end.

HUFC: Mawson, Travis, Mkandawire, James, Jeannin, Purdie, Pitman, Stanley, Brady, Williams, Ipoua. Subs: Beckwith, Lewis, Ferrell, Evans, Carey-Bertram.

ECFC: Jones, Woodwards, Sawyer, Jones, Todd, Afful, Taylor, Cronin, Challinor, Farrel, Mackie. Subs: Rice, Moxey, Watkins, Buckle, Flack.

Hereford United v Stockport County, 3 December 2005. Report by Brian Goodwin

United fail to make the grade

Hereford United were frustratingly knocked out of the F.A. Cup in the second round this afternoon at Edgar Street. Stockport County of League Two, who knocked out Swansea City in the first round, proved too strong for the Conference side as a goal in either half was enough to book The Hatters a place in round three.

Following the disappointing home defeat by Exeter last Saturday, Graham Turner made three changes to his side. Simon Travis was left out and Jon Brady found himself on the subs bench. Danny Carey-Bertram was rewarded with a start on the right and Adam Stansfield was named on the bench, as was Andy Bagnall who is under contract at Birmingham City.

Stockport didn't hesitate and came straight at Hereford from the start, resulting in an early lead for the visitors. An uncommon error from Tamika Mkandawire was a costly one, as he was out-muscled by Jermaine Easter, who raced clear of the defence and saw his shot

Hereford United v Stockport County FA CUP.
A WARM WELCOME... For Ex Hereford United left back Mark Robinson as he greets former team mate Rob Purdie. Robinson and his Stockport County team mates had the last laugh beating the Bulls 0-2 in the FA Cup.

rattle the cross bar before planting itself in the back of the net with just two minutes gone. This though, was about the only effort on Herefords' goal in the first half as United held out against their League Two opponents.

A corner was flapped at by 'keeper James Spencer giving Mkandawire a chance to shoot, his effort was blocked but Guy Ipoua sliced his volley wide of the mark as the ball made its way to the far post. Andy Williams believed he had a good penalty shout when he turned his defender, after receiving Jamie Pitman's pass, and then fell to the ground while under pressure from the towering presence of Michael Raynes but referee Mr. Singh didn't agree. United's best of the half came when Ipoua met Ryan Greens' cross with a volley that flashed wide of the near post. Williams had a snap shot just before the break but a deflection took the sting out of the ball and it was comfortable for Spencer.

Hereford United v Stockport County FA CUP.
Hereford's Alex Jeannin is challenged by Stockport County defenders Michael Raynes and Ross Greenwood.

Hereford United v Stockport County FA CUP.
Stockport goalkeeper James Spencer collects a cross under the challenge of Hereford forward Andrew Williams.

Hereford's Rob Purdie takes on two Stockport County midfielders during the Bulls 2-0 defeat in the FA Cup.

The Bulls almost equalised soon after the restart when Williams hit Carey-Bertram's low cross towards goal but Spencer made a good save from close range and the 'keeper was back on his feet in time to gather Rob Purdie's follow up shot. County made a rare attack and should gave wrapped the game up when Danny Boshell got in behind the defence, centred the ball only to see Craig Mawson deny a goal, as three attackers lined up but minutes later their place was booked in the third round after a spectacular goal.

The ball was turned into the air off a defenders leg and Mickael Wolski met the dropping ball with a thunderous volley from thirty yards, that flew past the helpless Mawson and into the bottom corner, much to the delight of the 586 away fans. Stockport almost grabbed a third a minute later but Mawson was able to block Harpal Singh's shot from the left of the box and as the visitors began to take full control of the game they were rewarded with a penalty, soon after Ipoua had been replaced by Stansfield.

Alex Jeannin was late with his challenge on Matthew Hamshaw and the ref duly pointed to the spot. Easter stepped up confidently but Mawson guessed correctly and palmed the ball into the path of Boshell, who shot harmlessly over. Williams was gifted with United's only other chance as they tried, but failed miserably, to make a comeback when he intercepted a pass across the defence but his shot was deflected behind. Brady was introduced late on but to little effect.

Stockport were, as their league position suggests, poor but in truth Hereford were worse. There was little attacking flair or pace and yet another defensive error proved vital. The majority of the 3,620 crowd will have been very disappointed with the performance of the hosts in what was seen as a great chance to book themselves a place in the third round and perhaps a money spinning tie.

HUFC: Mawson, Green, James, Mkandawire, Jeannin, Purdie, Stanley, Pitman, Carey-Bertram, Ipoua, Williams. Subs: Beckwith, Bagnall, Ferrell, Brady, Stansfield.

SCFC: Spencer, Greenwood, Clare, Raynes, Robinson, Singh, Wolski, Boshell, Hamshaw, Easter, Bramble. Subs: Duncan, Crowe, Ashley Williams, Allen, Malcolm.

Super Sub Sinks City

Adam Stansfield came off the subs bench and made an immediate impact as Hereford United claimed all three points in a scrappy encounter against York City. Graham Turner made several changes, five in total, to freshen up the side following last weeks unacceptable performance against Stockport. There was still no place for Simon Travis and Tony James, Jamie Pitman, Andy Williams and Craig Mawson were all dropped to the bench. Danny Carey-Bertram was not even amongst the substitutes.

Craig Stanley had found Graham Evans early on but he miss hit his shot and it flew harmlessly wide. James Dudgeon headed narrowly over for York before Guy Ipoua showed some fantastic skill to help himself past three defenders but he fired over. The Minstermen's top scorer Clayton Donaldson was the most threatening player to the United goal and almost broke the deadlock with a shot from thirty yards, but Wayne Brown managed to tip it inches over the bar.

Jon Brady and Ipoua linked up well to win a first in a spell of four successive corners. Tamika Mkandawire came closest from the third, which he met well with his head but 'keeper David Stockdale managed to get a hand to it. Levent Yalcin shot just over as York ended the first half with the better of the goal scoring chances.

Andy Ferrell miss cued soon after the restart as did Rob Purdie before Mkandawire beat the 'keeper with a header, from a free kick, but couldn't find the target as The Bulls began to look dangerous. Ferrell should have given United the lead but headed over from close range having got on the end of Brady's hooked cross while at the other end stand-in-skipper Mkandawire gave the crowd a scare when a through ball evaded him and Joe O'Neil chipped just over the bar.

Hereford United v York City

Hereford United player Adam Stansfield celebrates his winning goal against York City as team mates Andy Ferrell and Guy Ipoua rub his boot!!

Hereford United v York City

NOT THIS TIME... Hereford goalscorer Adam Stansfield just fails to block a clearance by York City right back Lee Andrews.

Hereford United v York City
A stunning save from York City 'keeper David Stockdale denies Hereford's Guy Ipoua.

Hereford finally broke through with twenty one minutes remaining when Stansfield netted for the first time this season. Just two minutes after his introduction he controlled Stanley's cross on his chest and, with his back to the goal, unleashed an awesome shot into the far top corner leaving Stockdale helpless. Stansfield was again involved just minutes later when Hereford should have put the game beyond doubt. He nodded the ball on to Ipoua, who beat his man, before seeing his low shot saved by the legs of the goalie. Purdie then hit the rebound wide with just a couple of defenders covering the goal.

Andy Williams came on to give the hosts a whole new-look strike force with ten minutes to go as York put the United defence under some pressure, which was dealt with well. Dean Beckwith and man of the match Ferrell stood out in the defensive roles. Hereford were able to break away more often now and almost got a second as a result of a break down the left which started and finished with Stansfield as he turned Purdie's cross over from close range. There was one last scare for the majority in the crowd of 1,950 in injury time though. Mark Convery struck the foot of the post following a centred ball from the right, much to the frustration of the 127 in the travelling army.

Graham Turner will be much more happy with his sides performance this week, having slammed his team following their F.A. Cup exit.

Hereford United v York City
Hereford's Rob Purdie cleverly evades a tackle from York City's Lee Andrews.

His changes paid off and he will also be delighted that Stansfield had an immediate impact when he came on. Despite the game being a scrappy one, not helped by a card happy referee, United will be much more content after this game.

HUFC: Brown, Green, Beckwith, Mkandawire, Jeannin, Purdie, Stanley, Ferrell, Brady, Ipoua, Evans. Subs: Mawson, James, Pitman, Williams, Stansfield.

YCFC: Stockdale, Andrews, McGurk, Dudgeon, Bertos, Yalcin, Barwick, Dunning, Horwood, O'Neill, Donaldson. Subs: Hotte, Price, Porter, Convery, Stewart.

Bognor Regis v Hereford United, 17 December 2005. Report by Organic Bull
(Bulls News was unable to provide a full report for this game)

Bognor on the Rocks after Bulls score Seven

Hereford United will receive £4,000 for defeating Bognor Regis 7-1 this afternoon in the FA Trophy First Round game.

Andy Williams put the Bulls ahead after five minutes. He cut inside from the right and finished with a left foot shot from about 25 yards.

Second goal for the Bulls came on fourteen minutes from Adam Stansfield who ran through the inside left channel before shooting with his right foot from around the edge of the box.

Bognor replied three minutes later when Dan Beck turned the ball into the goal from close quarters.

The home side have had two penalty appeals turned down.

Half Time: Bognor Regis 1, Hereford United 2

Andy Ferrell was been booked for a late challenge early in the second half.

Hereford were awarded a penalty for hand-ball on 62 minutes. Rob Purdie got the ball into the back of the net but the referee told him to take it again. This time Purdie converted into the top corner.

Craig Stanley booked for dissent.

Guy Ipoua, after a good run, made it 4-0. Stanley made it five from ten yards out just two minutes later.

Jamie Pitman replaced Ipoua as Williams moved up-front with Stansfield.

Purdie made it six after the Rocks goalkeeper made a meal of clearing a shot.

On 84 minutes Pitman made it seven with a lob over the top of the goalkeeper.

Graham Evans and Danny Carey-Bertram came on late as subs.

This report was compiled from various sources.

Line up: Mawson, Travis, Mkandawire, Beckwith, Jeannin, Purdie, Ferrell, Stanley, Williams, Ipoua and Stansfield.

Subs: Bagnell, Evans , James, Pitman and Carey-Bertram.

Hereford United v Scunthorpe United, 20 December 2005. Report by Brian Goodwin

Super Bulls cruise past Scunny

A brilliant first half performance was the base for Hereford Uniteds' latest league scalp in the LDV Vans Trophy. Scunthorpe United were the visitors to Edgar Street this evening and were the third league team that the Bulls have knocked out of the cup. It was the second time in as many seasons that The Iron have been defeated in this competition by The Bulls.

Craig Stanley and Dean Beckwith were the only two changes to the starting line-up while there was no place for Danny

Hereford United v Scunthorpe United
LDV Vans Quarter Final

Hereford goalscorer Adam Stansfield has his point blank shot blocked by Scunthorpe goalkeeper Tom Evans.

Carey-Bertram on the bench. Tony James was handed his place back in defence and Jamie Pitman lined up alongside Andy Ferrell in the midfield. The hosts made their intentions clear from the off, as they came straight at their League One opponents and had won a corner within a minute.

It was from a Scunny corner though, that Hereford's first real chance came from. A dangerous ball was delivered into the Bulls' box but, after a scramble, they countered through Simon Travis and his cross was inches away from the threatening foot of Adam Stansfield. Cleveland Taylor worked a good opening with some neat skill past James but his shot was well saved by Craig Mawson before rebounding out for a corner off Pitman.

Hereford continued to attack and took the lead with just seventeen minutes gone. Ferrell crossed in from the right and it was Rob Purdie who beat the offside trap to take the ball down, seemingly with his arm, but his low effort was pushed away by the 'keeper, but Stansfield was on hand to turn the loose ball into the open net. Guy Ipoua almost added to the lead moments after, when Pitman centred the ball and the Cameroonian hit the foot of the post from the edge of the box.

Purdie forced another save out of Tom Evans, this time from thirty yards out and once again the ball was played into the path of Stansfield but Evans was able to recover and force a corner this time. Alex Jeannin managed to hit the post from the resulting corner and then, in almost comical fashion, Evans was almost beaten by one of his own defenders who nearly lobbed him from twenty five yards out.

Stansfield, who has now scored three goals in as many games, was again at the heart of

Hereford United v Scunthorpe United
LDV Vans Quarter Final

Hereford goalscorers Adam Stansfield and Tamika Mkandawire challenge Scunthorpe's Ian Barraclough and Cleveland Taylor.

Hereford United v Scunthorpe United LDV Vans Quarter Final
Hereford players celebrate Tamika Mkandawire's goal against Scunthorpe watched by referee Andy Woolmer.

yet another Hereford attack, as he broke away down the right and delivered a perfect cross to the far post. Purdie, having made a decent connection with it, managed to hit the cross bar with his volley from little more than two yards with five minutes of the half remaining. Before the break there was time for the infamous referee Andy Woolmer to make yet another poor decision, in what was another poor performance from him. Stansfield was clearly tripped in the penalty area but Woolmer waved claims away.

However, Hereford did manage to net a second before the break as Tamika Mkandawire rose to direct an unstoppable header into the back of the net from Purdie's corner. In injury time, Ipoua slid a well timed through ball into Stansfield, but he managed to slice his effort wide while one on one with Evans. James had pulled up with an injury by now, and was duly replaced by Dean Beckwith at the half time break.

The second period was a lot less eventful than the first, but it was inevitable that either side would not be able to keep up the pace that had been set. It was the home side who continued to look the most threatening though as the game became scrappy. Ferrell had found Andy Williams with a brilliant cross-field pass and Williams cut inside before shooting inches wide of the far post, where Stansfield almost turned the ball over the line.

The Iron responded by introducing their first choice strike force with Steve Torpey and top scorer Billy Sharp replacing Tommy Johnson and Wayne Cordon but man of the match Mkandawire, who was a rock in the brilliant Hereford defence throughout, and Beckwith kept the two very quiet indeed. Another Hereford counter attack almost resulted in another goal, but, following good play between Williams, Ipoua and Purdie, Stansfield sliced wide when in on goal, again!

Scunny did have a little spell towards the end of the game where they forced Mawson into some work, firstly when Andy Keogh shot from twenty five yards and the Hereford 'keeper pushed the ball over the bar. Soon after Keogh played Sharp in on goal, but Mawson was quickly out at Keogh's feet to block with his legs. The ball fell to Keogh, whose shot was blocked by the head of Pitman and then it was Torpey to have a go, but his header was brilliantly turned behind by the goalie.

United managed to play out the remaining five or so minutes with little trouble and Graham Evans was introduced late on in place of Adam Stansfield. His strike partner Ipoua had earlier been replaced by Jon Brady as a precaution, as it seemed he was risking a second yellow card from Woolmer.

It was a thoroughly entertaining encounter in which Hereford, for the most part, were the better side. Their first half display was about the best forty five minutes of football played by The Bulls this season and was clearly enjoyed by the majority of the crowd of 1,452, which included 57 away fans. The result follows up nicely from the cup success at Bognor Regis and sets Hereford up nicely for the Christmas Period. There is also a possibility that they could have a tasty Northern Section Semi-Final tie against local rivals Kidderminster Harriers.

THE RED CARD TREATMENT... For referee Andy Woolmer who received a cool reception from Hereford United fans as he took charge of the LDV Vans Quarter Final against Scunthorpe. Woolmer returned to Edgar Street for the first time after causing controversy after sending Bulls centre back Andy Tretton off in the vital play off with Aldershot the season before last. Fans waved red cards to the official before during and after the game. The picture shows a card dropped towards the official (2nd right) as he left the pitch.

HUFC: Mawson, Travis, Mkandawire, James, Jeannin, Purdie, Pitman, Ferrell, Williams, Ipoua, Stansfield. Subs: Beckwith, Lewis, Stanley, Evans, Brady.

SUFC: Evans, Goodwin, Byrne, Crosby, Ridley, Taylor, Baraclough, MacKenzie, Corden, Keogh, Johnson. Subs: Musselwhite, Torpey, Till, Ryan, Sharp.

Forest Green Rovers v Hereford United, 26 December 2005. Report by Brian Goodwin

Bulls stumble at The Lawn

Hereford United failed to continue their recent impressive form as they could only manage a draw at lowly Forest Green Rovers. Graham Turner had to make a couple of forced changes, so Darren Blewitt started along side Tamika Mkandawire at the back as Dean Beckwith was banned and Tony James was injured. Andy Ferrell was also out injured and so Craig Stanley regained his starting place.

Julian Alsop was a constant threat for Rovers, as he troubled the United defence with his height and strength, which resembled Forest Green's general style. Their physical approach disrupted The Bulls' game as they struggled to make anything of the first half.

Alsop was first to threaten, but he headed wide before Stanley, Adam Stanfield and Rob Purdie all had efforts, which came to nothing.

Paul Wanless came close to breaking the deadlock with twenty minutes gone, when he found himself with some space just ten yards out. Unmarked, he controlled a cross into the box but saw his low drive beaten away by the on-rushing Craig Mawson. Fifteen minutes later though, Mawson was beaten. It was against the run of play, but Green countered well on the miss positioned Alex Jeannin, who'd just been involved in an attack. Alex Meechan paced away down the left, from just inside the Hereford half, turned Mkandawire and fired beyond the reach of the advancing Mawson and into the bottom corner.

After the restart, United came out with renewed hope and started to pressure the hosts again, and it paid off little more than ten minutes into the half. Purdie delivered a free kick into the box and Mkandawire out-jumped 'keeper Ryan Clarke and looped a header into the far corner for the equaliser. Guy Ipoua then burst into life as The Bulls searched for the lead and the Cameroonian should have netted when he controlled Andy Williams' cross, but was denied by a smart save. Moments later, he superbly turned his man on the edge of the box but fired against the cross bar.

Just as it seemed that Forest Green had weathered the storm, Alex Jeannin put Hereford in front with a goal, pretty much, out of nothing. The Frenchman played a one-two with Purdie and lobbed Clarke with a wonderful twenty yard volley, much to the delight of the 1,000 or so away fans. However, their jubilation was short lived, as they paid for a lapse in concentration and Rovers were level again just two minutes later.

Super-sub Guy Madjo, who didn't start because he turned up to the game late (a good thing for United, as he caused plenty of problems when introduced), latched onto a long ball and held off Mkandawire and Jeannin before firing a well placed half volley into the bottom corner from the edge of the box. Hereford tried take the lead for a second time but couldn't create a lot in the remaining ten minutes, and it was Madjo again who almost stole a winner for the hosts in injury time, but Mawson was out quickly to deny him the chance.

All in all, it was a very disappointing afternoon for Hereford at The Lawn, as they would have fully expected to take all three points at the start of the afternoon. A lacklustre first half performance meant that they had it all to do in the second half, and it was a lapse in concentration that spoilt their second half efforts as, other than the goal, they were rarely troubled in the second period. The attendance of 1,957 was the highest of the season for Rovers, in which the home fans were seemingly outnumbered by the away supporters.

HUFC: Mawson, Travis, Mkandawire, Blewitt, Jeannin, Purdie, Stanley, Pitman, Williams, Ipoua, Stansfield. Subs: Gwynne, Brady, Brown, Evans, Carey-Bertram.

FGRFC: Clarke, Simpson, Richardson, Graham, Searle, Meechan, Gadsby, Wanless, Harding, Alsop, Teixeira. Subs: Harrison, Rogers, Rendell, Garner, Madjo.

Exeter City v Hereford United, 30 December 2005. Report by Brian Goodwin

Perfect Day For AJ

Not only did his side win, but he scored against his former team in front of his former fans, all on his birthday! Not a bad day for Alex Jeannin and Hereford United as they claimed a well earned 2-1 victory against Exeter City at St. James' Park this evening, in front of Sky TV cameras.

The two sides met a month ago at Edgar Street when Exeter emerged 2-0 victors but this time it was Hereford's turn to take all three points. The Bulls lined up with two changes from the starting eleven that took a point at Forest Green on Boxing Day, as Dean Beckwith returned from suspension and started in place of Darren Blewitt. However, it was Beckwith who was at fault as the hosts took an early lead following a good start. The centre back hesitated on clearing a long ball forward and in nipped Lee Phillips to pace into the box and fire a powerful low shot across Wayne Brown, back in goal at the expense of Craig Mawson, and into the far bottom corner.

Craig Farral had already forced Brown into a save, following a long throw-in and The Grecians continued their domination when Jon Challinor met a left-wing cross on the volley, but couldn't direct it on target. Adam Stansfield had forced a corner moments earlier in a rare Bull's attack, as passes went astray from the Hereford midfield and so Exeter were enjoying the majority of play. Jeannin almost gifted his former side a second goal when he sliced a clearance in the box, allowing Glenn Cronin to intercept but he shot against the cross bar.

On the half-hour mark though, Guy Ipoua turned the game around with a wonderful goal completely against the run of play. Jamie Pitman, who'd not been on the top of his game, played a ball into the feet of Ipoua who superbly turned his man, went around another player and fired into the top corner from outside of the box for a wonderful superb equaliser. United grew in confidence from then on and started attacking Exeter more and causing them problems. Stansfield chased down and blocked Paul Jones' clearance, which fell to Ipoua but he fired inches wide.

Stansfield was again causing problems for the defence and was tripped twenty five yards from goal with just two minutes of the half remaining. Pitman touched the ball on and, as though it was scripted, Jeannin placed a peach of a shot into the far top corner to put United 2-1 up. Hereford's celebrations were short lived, one again, though as before the game had restarted Ipoua had been shown the red-card, for no reason clear to most in the crowd. It's being said that he made an "obscene gesture" to the Exeter crowd, although it's thought that the referee may have miss interpreted Ipoua's actions. So Hereford were in front, but down to ten men, with a whole half to go.

Hereford came out and continued to attack The Grecians in the second half, somewhat surprisingly, and Andy Williams burst into the box early on and seemed to have his legs taken from underneath him, but no penalty was given despite appeals. Craig Stanley helped the ball on, following another good run from Williams, to Stansfield and his shot from a narrow angle went just inches wide of the far post, having beaten Jones. Gary Sawyer came close for the hosts at the other end when he headed a corner just wide but United had been the better side after the restart.

Both sides made a number of changes, the first after sixty-five minutes being when target man Steve Flack was introduced for Exeter when they had just won a corner. United cleared their lines broke quickly through Williams, who knocked a good ball down the line for Stansfield and he outpaced the defenders but was denied by Jones when one on one, as he fired in a low shot. Blewitt replaced Beckwith for Hereford, maybe to deal with the extra threat of Flack, or maybe because Beckwith has been suffering with illness while Santos Gaia and Dean Moxey came on for the hosts. Carey-Bertram replaced Stansfield as the single Hereford striker with less than ten minutes to go.

It was Carey-Bertram who had the perfect chance to seal all three points when he was played through on goal but he was twice denied by Jones, who got down to both of the efforts well. Exeter pumped long ball into the

Hereford box but didn't get the goal they so badly wanted, although Danny Woodards came extremely close when he headed over from close range, with Brown already beaten by the cross.

The brilliant result, in front of 4,433 (with around 130 Bulls supporters) means that Hereford move up one place to sixth, and they are now two points outside of the play offs, although they have a game in hand on some sides above them. Exeter are seven points better off than The Bulls, in second place, but have played two more games.

HUFC: Brown, Travis, Mkandawire, Beckwith, Jeannin, Purdie, Pitman, Stanley, Williams, Stansfield, Ipoua. Subs: Blewitt, Mawson, Brady, Evans, Carey-Bertram.

ECFC: Paul Jones, Woodards, Todd, Sawyer, Billy Jones, Taylor, Buckle, Cronin, Challinor, Farrell, Phillips. Subs: Gaia, Rice, Moxey, Mackie, Flack.

Hereford United v Forest Green Rovers, 2 January 2006. Report by Brian Goodwin

Madjo pegs Bulls back again

Guy Madjo starred and got the equaliser, once again, as Forest Green Rovers came from behind to draw with Hereford United for the second time this Christmas period. Both sides had notched up impressive victories on the weekend and having drawn a week ago, the pre-match form gave the impression of a good game to come.

Hereford were unchanged from the side that started against Exeter other than Ryan Green being named on the bench as Darren Blewitt's loan spell with the club has ended. United continued from where they left off against The Grecians and came out at Rovers, and dominated the opening half. Guy Ipoua found Andy Williams to the right of the box

Forest Green Rovers goalkeeper Ryan Clarke punches clear a Hereford United attack.

Hereford United v Forest Green Rovers.
Hereford United defender Dean Beckwith shadows Forest Greens Julian Alsop

Hereford United v Forest Green Rovers.
Forest Green Rovers goalkeeper Ryan Clarke collects a cross above Hereford United's Guy Ipoua.

for The Bull's first chance, and the youngster turned inside his man only to see his low shot saved by Ryan Clarke.

Although in almost complete control, United were finding it difficult to break through the Forest Green defence. Rob Purdie was threatening with the ball at his feet but was severely lacking when it came to the end product. The hosts then enjoyed a spell where the won three consecutive corners, but at the end of it Rovers broke through Madjo, who found Ben Harding but he directed his effort just the wrong side of the far post. Harding again went close soon after, but once again just missed the target before the deadlock was broken on the half hour mark.

Hereford United v Forest Green Rovers.
Hereford United striker Adam Stansfield is congratulated by team mates Jamie Pitman and Dean Beckwith after scoring against Forest Green Rovers.

United had a free kick twenty yards out and Pitman centred it for Alex Jeannin to run onto. The pass was closed down, forcing Jeannin to side-step the defender before unleashing a powerful effort that was parried away by Clarke. Adam Stansfield was the quickest to react to it and he managed to turn it into the corner of the net from ten yards out. United continued to have the better of things, but didn't come close again before half time, other than when Stansfield was beaten to a ball over the top from Williams, by Clarke, who headed into the path of Craig Stanley. Stanley looked up to see an open goal, but shot just wide from thirty five yards out.

The first had been a poor encounter in truth, so it was hoped that things would improve in the second. Forest Green looked the more dangerous of the two sides though, and Madjo, a constant threat, almost levelled things up when he met Harding's free kick with his head, but could only direct it straight at Wayne Brown. However, with just under an hour gone, Madjo finally got the better of Brown and his defence. He muscled off the challenge from Dean Beckwith as a high ball came into the box, turned well and slotted the ball in, albeit via the inside of the post, from inside the six yard area with the angle against him.

Purdie had a tame shot saved easily as United really struggled in the final third against a stern and strong defence and so, with twenty five minutes remaining, Graham Turner made a triple substitution. Green, Danny Carey-Bertram and Jon Brady were introduced in place of Pitman, Stansfield and Williams. Green was sent on in centre midfield, a position that he is not familiar with. Stansfield will have been disappointed to be replaced when he'd been far more effective than Ipoua.

Carey-Bertram had a shot on the turn blocked, following a cross from man of the match Jeannin who'd been set away down the left flank from a good ball by Stanley while at the other end Alex Meechan had crossed just beyond Madjo at the far post. Carey-Bertram shot over from twenty yards following a break through the middle from Green and a final chance fell to Purdie in the box, but his effort was deflected behind for a corner.

The final whistle ended a disappointing Christmas period for The Bulls, as they collected just five points from a possible nine. The midfield seems to be an area where Hereford were poor, not for the first time, today and with the transfer window now open, it would be no surprise if Turner was to invest in a centre midfielder. With other results generally going in Herefords' favour, they fall just once place to seventh. They will be hoping to make some ground back up next Saturday when they travel to Scarborough, a side struggling in the league, like Forest Green have been.

HUFC: Brown, Travis, Mkandawire, Beckwith, Jeannin, Purdie, Pitman, Stanley, Williams, Stansfield, Ipoua. Subs: Green, Mawson, Brady, Evans, Carey-Bertram.

FGRFC: Clarke, Simpson, Alsop, Richardson, Graham, Searle, Gadsby, Wanless, Harding, Meechan, Madjo. Subs: Garner, Sall, Teixeira, Rendell, Harrison.

Scarborough v Hereford United, 7 January 2006. Report by Brian Goodwin

United scrap for victory at Scarborough

Hereford United took all three points at the McCain Stadium this afternoon following a scrappy encounter with Scarborough, who are struggling in the lower reaches of the table. Both teams went into the game off the back of draws but Hereford's league position made them obvious favourites.

United made two changes to the side; Darryl Taylor, spending his second loan spell in two seasons with United, was in the side at the expense of Andy Williams and Danny Carey-Bertram started alongside Adam Stansfield, as Guy Ipoua was missing through injury.

Brian Wake headed towards goal but caused Wayne Brown no problems early on before Neil Bishop fired inches wide from twenty yards. At the other end Alex Jeannin hit a free kick straight down the middle of the goal before Stansfield netted the first and only goal of the game. Craig Stanley hooked a ball over the top of the defence from inside of his own half and Stansfield raced ahead of his marker and poked the ball beyond the reach of Leigh Walker and into the back of the net, with eleven minutes gone.

The Seadogs replied, forcing Brown into an excellent save, as he tipped a header of Tony Hackworth just around the post while, at the other end, Tamika Mkandawire looped a header onto the top of the crossbar. Wake, ever dangerous for the hosts, broke through the Hereford rear-guard, but over-hit a ball just to his left where Bishop awaited, when he was in a good scoring position himself, and the ball ran out for a goal kick. In injury time, Boro almost got the equaliser they were searching for, but Sean McClare volleyed inches wide from just inside the area.

Wake continued to look Scarborough's most likely scorer, and shot just wide of the far post from long range after the restart, in what was, again, a poor half for both sides. Wake was subbed off after sixty four minutes, which was probably a relief to United's defence. Five minutes later Williams was introduced in place of Carey-Bertram as both sides struggled to create opportunities. Michael Coulson, Wake's replacement, forced the first save of the half from Brown having twisted and turned on the edge of the box before firing in low.

Rob Purdie, who was not enjoying his best of games, played a neat ball down the line for Williams, who skinned his opponent and won a corner, as his cross was nodded behind at the near post. Mkandawire, who had already came close due to his aerial threat, met the corner with a glancing header, which fell just inches wide of the far post. Ryan Green was given the final quarter of an hour to impress, as he took Simon Travis' place at right back, but despite the fresh legs in defence, Boro began piling on the pressure.

United's back line was standing strong though, but Coulson almost found an equaliser when he collected a head down in the box, after it was lofted in from a free kick, but fired wide from a central position. Graham Turner introduced Graham Evans late on and he did manage to get the ball into the back of the net, but it was disallowed by the referee.

The victory, which despite the rather poor performance is what matters at the end of the day, means that The Bulls move up to fifth in the league, into the play off positions. United once again lacked an attacking threat throughout, although man of the match Stansfield put full effort in, yet again, and Taylor did well on the right. However he did look out of match practice which was noticeable as he failed, on more than one occasion, to deliver a good cross having made himself plenty of space.

Around 100 Hereford supporters travelled to Scarborough in a crowd of 1,582, although it looked at least a couple of hundred less!

HUFC: Brown, Travis, Beckwith, Mkandawire, Jeannin, Purdie, Stanley, Pitman, Taylor, Carey-Bertram, Stansfield. Subs: Green, Mawson, Gwynne, Williams, Evans.

SFC: Walker, Ingram, Baker, Atkinson, Lyth, Bishop, Hughes, McClare, Nicholson, Hackworth, Wake. Subs: Dunbavin, Quayle, Foot, Coulson, Weaver.

Halifax Town Football Club v Hereford United, 14 January 2006. Report by Brian Goodwin

United Creep Past The Shaymen

Hereford United crept into the final 16 of the F.A. Trophy with a 1-0 victory against Halifax at The Shay this afternoon. A single goal separated the two teams in an un-entertaining cup tie which was probably not considered all too important by either side. The Bulls made a few changes to their side; Wayne Brown was out cup tied, and so Craig Mawson deputised, Craig Stanley missed out through suspension and Danny Carey-Bertram was dropped to the bench meaning starts for Andy Williams and Andy Ferrell.

Halifax started the better side with Danny Forest shooting over via a deflection winning a corner for the hosts, but United netted with their first attack of the game, inspired by Williams. The youngster played a neat ball down the left flank for Adam Stansfield who turned his marker and found Williams just inside the penalty area. Williams turned before driving in a low shot, which was pushed away by Adam Legzdins, but Stansfield was on hand to convert the rebound.

Lewis Killeen shot wide of the mark as Halifax tried to pull level while, at the other end, Williams played an inviting ball across the goal face which Stansfield couldn't quite stretch to before the first half was drawn to a close. The second period was perhaps more eventful, but still rather poor spectacle, at least in the early stage. Dean Beckwith picked up a booking for a foul just outside the box, and Martin Foster struck the resulting free kick over the bar before Chris Senior saw a shot from a tight angle saved by Mawson.

Matt Doughty had a free kick saved as Halifax continued to dominate, restricting Hereford to rare attacks which more often than not came to nothing. Adam Quinn smashed an effort towards goal, but man of the match Beckwith got in the way of it and deflected the ball out for a corner. Daryl Taylor was replaced by Carey-Bertram, and Graham Turner switched to a 4-5-1 formation with Stansfield working alone up front.

Alex Jeannin, who had a very poor match, struck a free kick over for The Bulls in what was a rare attempt at goal while Beckwith again blocked well, this time denying Killeen. Halifax tried lofting balls into Hereford's box but the defence seemed to deal with them fairly well, and as the game came to a close, United looked more and more likely to snatch a second on the break.

The performance seemed to resemble that of last weekends trip to Scarborough, where Hereford went 1-0 up and then worked hard to defend that lead, which they once again did successfully. However, it was not the most pleasing spectacle for the 100 or so supporters who made the trip in the crowd of 1,220.

HUFC: Mawson, Travis, Mkandawire, Beckwith, Jeannin, Purdie, Pitman, Ferrell, Taylor, Williams, Stansfield. Subs: Green, Gwynne, Evans, Carey-Bertram.

HTFC: Legzdins, Haslam, Doughty, Quinn, Foster, Killeen, Thompson, Atherton, Grant, Forrest, Prendergast. Subs: Bushell, Midgley, Senior, Young, Jacobs.

Hereford United v Crawley Town, 21 January 2006. Report by Brian Goodwin

Guy Delivers the Goods

Hereford United took all three points as they stole a late victory against Crawley Town this afternoon and completed a double over The Red Devils for this season. Crawley, who started the day just outside of the relegation zone, are now in 20th place and Hereford, who started just outside of the play offs, are now in 4th position.

Graham Turner made a couple of changes from the side that beat Halifax in the F.A. Trophy last week as Wayne Brown returned as did Craig Stanley, who'd been suspended. He played on the right wing and there was no place for loanee Daryl Taylor who was injured. Guy Ipoua was also recalled to the bench following an injury, as was Tony James.

Although the game started slowly, United had the lead with just seven minutes gone. Adam Stansfield and Andy Williams had worked well in a small space on the edge of the box when the ball, off a Crawley defender, slipped into the box where Williams was ahead of the defence, and the youngster showed good composure to round Phil Smith

Hereford United v Crawley Town
GOAL… Crawley Town goalkeeper Phil Smith is left helpless as Guy Ipoua's header loops over him.

in the Crawley goal and slot Hereford into the lead.

Crawley were looking suspect in defence but were also threatening going forward. Their industrious approach often troubled United and the strike pairing of Steve Burton and Chris Giles worked well. The visitors should have levelled things up when Dean Beckwith was unable to control a long ball forward, allowing Giles to sprint clear but he fired wide when one on one with Brown. Tamika Mkandawire almost doubled the lead when he connected with Alex Jeannin's corner on the volley, but his effort was blocked. Rob Purdie had hit the side netting for The Bulls before he was taken off with six minutes of the half remaining. Purdie had not been enjoying the best of games but it was later revealed that he'd been ill. Danny Carey-Bertram came on to play on the wing.

Crawley came out for the second half looking much better and more threatening than in the first half. They began to dominate in the midfield, where Jamie Pitman had excelled in the first period, with Danny Brown's tenacious work and the creativity of Tony Scully. It was the ever-threatening Giles though who came close from a corner which he met well but Brown managed to tip over the bar. He again went close soon after with his head again, but his time was denied by the cross bar.

The visitors continued to peg Hereford back and finally got their reward midway through the second half. Adam Stansfield, who seemed to be limping, was replaced by Guy Ipoua just after the hour mark and just two minutes later Crawley drew level. They'd almost scored a minute before following a counter attack, as they quickly cleared a Hereford corner but United managed to get just enough men back. The goal was a thunderous effort, as Danny Brown picked up a loose ball thirty yards from goal and unleashed a powerful effort which flashed into the bottom corner, leaving Wayne Brown standing helpless in the Hereford goal.

Hereford United v Crawley Town
HIGH FLIERS… Crawley Town's Tony Scully and Hereford United's Jamie Pitman.

Hereford United v Crawley Town
GOAL… Hereford United striker Guy Ipoua heads in the winner against Crawley.

Hereford were triggered into action and produced their first real attacking incentives of the second half but Carey-Bertram's cross was just beyond Williams at the far post and it was Crawley who then enjoyed another good spell, in which Ben Judge saw a long range effort held by Brown. United again tried to get back into the game but didn't look like creating much and it looked as though this would not be their day. It was the visitors who looked more likely to go on to take all three points.

However, Stanley had won a free kick on the right which Jeannin delivered into the box but it was returned to him. While some were appealing for a hand ball decision, Jeannin had crossed again and Ipoua met it with his head, but it fell just the wrong side of the post. He made amends for the miss with just two minutes left on the clock. Carey-Bertram crossed from the left this time and Ipoua, from fifteen yards out, managed somehow to get enough power from his header to loop the ball over Smith in front of a relieved Meadow End.

The Bulls almost put the result beyond any doubt in the fourth and final added minute

Hereford United v Crawley Town
Hereford United's Andy Williams (left) celebrates scoring against Crawley with fellow striker Adam Stansfield.

when Pitman released Carey-Bertram on the left flank. He cut inside and raced through on goal, but his low effort was saved by the legs of the 'keeper. It didn't matter though, and United took the three points much to the delight of the majority of the crowd of 2,782, which included 57 away fans. The result extends Hereford's unbeaten run to six Conference games and nine games in all competitions.

HUFC: Brown, Travis, Mkandawire, Beckwith, Jeannin, Purdie, Ferrell, Pitman, Stanley, Williams, Stansfield. Subs: Mawson, James, Evans, Carey-Bertram, Ipoua.

CTFC: Smith, Judge, Simpemba, Mendy, Opinel, Blackburn, Brown, Armstrong, Scully, Giles, Burton. Subs: Ward, Jenkins, Woozley, Ekoku, Whitman.

Macclesfield Town v Hereford United, 24 January 2006. Report by Brian Goodwin

Bulls stumble at semi-final stage again

Hereford United were knocked out of the LDV Vans Trophy last night by Macclesfield Town at Moss Lane. It is the second season in succession that The Bulls have been eliminated at the (Northern) area semi-final stage against League opposition.

United, without the injured Adam Stansfield and Stacey Coldicott, cup-tied Daryl Taylor and ineligible Wayne Brown, started with an unfamiliar 4-5-1 formation with Andy Williams and Danny Carey-Bertram occupying the wings. There was a recall to the starting eleven for Guy Ipoua, Craig Mawson and Carey-Bertram and Ryan Green returned from injury and was named amongst the substitutes.

The first half had rather and "end-to-end" style to it, but it was Macclesfield who were by far the happier of the two sides at the break, despite play having been fairly equal. The Silkmen always looked dangerous going forwards, with midfielders breaking quickly from the midfield, something that Hereford lacked, although Ipoua played well as the lone-striker. However, it was Martin Bullock in the centre who provided the first chance for the hosts. His through ball found Danny Whitaker but Mawson saved when the striker was through, and Tamika Mkandawire cleared for a corner.

Whitaker had been denied this time, but with nineteen minutes gone he broke the deadlock. He managed to force his way through the centre of Hereford's defence and left Mawson with no chance as he smashed home the opener from ten yards out. United put The Silkmen under some pressure but didn't trouble 'keeper Alan Fettis, even though Williams did well to put in some dangerous crosses from the right flank. At the other end Kevin Townson saw a shot deflected behind by Beckwith, but Hereford broke from the resulting corner through Pitman who supplied a good pass for Carey-Bertram, however he fired Hereford's only real shot of the half just wide.

There was still time left in the half, though, for The Silkmen to double their advantage after forty five minutes. Kevin McIntyre turned his man on the edge of the Bull's box and knocked the ball to his left where Paul Harsley fired into the top corner, again leaving Mawson with no chance. Graham Turner made a much needed change at the interval, with Rob Purdie replacing Andy Ferrell and he switched the formation to a 4-4-2 with Carey-Bertram joining Ipoua in attack.

The change in formation was an effective one as The Whites began to threaten much more. Ipoua, at the heart of nearly everything that United created, headed a Mawson goal kick on for Carey-Bertram who poked over from the left of the penalty box. Ipoua then fired inches wide as he showed good strength and power to burst through the centre of The Silkmen's defence and went closer again with a speculative effort from twenty five yards that flew just over the bar.

Williams headed wide from a Purdie corner as United again failed to force a save out of Fettis, but continued to peg their graded opponents back and limit them to very rare attacks on the break, which led to nothing. Craig Stanley played man of the match Ipoua through just ahead of the defence, but he was denied reasonably easily by Fettis while Mkandawire, still up from a corner late on, managed to turn his man in the box but the ball, that had been played just in front of him, was cleared by David Morley.

It was a disappointing result in the end for Hereford, who had good reason to feel that they had done enough to at least get a draw that would have taken the tie to extra-time. The first half ended up being decisive and it was the hosts who were much more prepared to gamble and send men forward from the midfield to support their front men who gained a place in the area final. Maybe if one of the three centre midfielders in Ferrell, Pitman, and Stanley, had given more support to Ipoua, who stood out throughout, then the result may have been different. The attendance was perhaps a little disappointing for the hosts, as they could only manage around 1,000 fans in a crowd of 1,315.

HUFC: Mawson, Travis, Mkandawire, Beckwith, Jeannin, Williams, Pitman, Ferrell, Stanley, Carey-Bertram, Ipoua. Subs: James, Lewis, Green, Evans, Purdie.

MTFC: Fettis, Swailes, Morley, Sandwith, Harsley, Whitaker, Navarro, McIntyre, Bullock, Wijnhard, Townson. Subs: Beresford, Lee, Teague, Miles, Smart

Grays Athletic v Hereford United, 28 January 2006. Report by Brian Goodwin

Purdie inspires Bulls comeback

Hereford United's second half performance earned them a deserved 2-2 draw at Grays Athletic this afternoon, having been two down at the interval. The sides, both hoping for at least a place in the play-offs by the end of the season, had met at Edgar Street earlier in the season when Grays were 2-0 victors and will meet again at Edgar Street in a weeks time in the F.A. Trophy.

Graham Turner started with new loan signing Nicky Nicolau on the left wing and with Rob Purdie in the centre of the midfield alongside Andy Ferrell. Craig Stanley was dropped to the bench and Jamie Pitman missed out through injury. Adam Stansfield recovered from a knock that kept him out of the LDV game in midweek and so Danny Carey-Bertram made way and Wayne Brown regained his spot in goal at the expense of Craig Mawson. Stacy Caldicott warmed up with the team but did not make the team sheet.

An entertaining opening to the half provided very little in goal scoring opportunities for either side, as both went looking for an early lead. Aaron McLean, infamous with Hereford supporters, forced Brown into his first save of the afternoon when he shot on the turn following a corner before Simon Travis had to be alert to get a block on Gary Hooper's shot, as he controlled well in the box. Alex Jeannin almost handed a goal to The Blues as he conceded possession to John Martin, but the strikers shot was saved. Moments previously, Guy Ipoua had been felled and with just 25 minutes gone was replaced by Carey-Bertram.

Three minutes later, The Bulls found themselves behind but will not be happy with the linesman, as there was a big question of offside in the build up. Michael Kightly spread the ball to the right flank where Hooper, who looked to be at least a yard ahead of the defence, cut the ball back from the by-line for McLean who netted, despite the attempt of Travis on the line. McLean then went over to the travelling army of around 350 (in a crowd of 1,528) and threw himself on the ground in celebration.

United responded well and created their first attempts on goal but could not get the equaliser. Nicolau found Stansfield who played the ball back into the box to his strike-partner Carey-Bertram who turned well before firing beyond Ashley Bayes in the Grays goal, but McLean was on the line to clear. The ball fell back to Carey-Bertram but he shot poorly straight at the grateful Bayes. To make matters worse, the hosts doubled their advantage minutes later. Again, United may feel a bit aggrieved at the manner of the goal as Dean Beckwith was harshly adjudged to have fouled on the edge of the box and was carded as a result. A rehearsed free kick was put into practice and Stuart Thurgood, instrumental throughout, placed delicately into the bottom corner. The ball didn't carry much pace by Brown, who appeared to go for the ball and then stop, couldn't reach it as it crept into the corner of the net. So United, for the second game in a row, were two down at the break.

The Bulls came out for the second half with renewed belief and pegged Grays back from the start, although again they didn't create much in the way of goal scoring opportunities. Purdie was brimming with effort and was very effective in the centre midfield role. He was obviously far happier there than on the left wing where he's found himself for the most part of the season. Ferrell had blazed over as United continued to pressure in a rare effort at goal and Stansfield headed harmlessly onto the roof of the net before Travis almost put the game on a plate for the hosts. His header, intended for Brown, was played directly in the path of Hooper, but the youngster blasted over when one on one.

And four minutes later, United made Hooper pay for his miss. Following a corner, Beckwith received the ball in the midfield area and toed a pass down the left to Jeannin. He delivered an inch perfect cross into the area, where Mkandawire, still up from the corner, came out of nowhere and smashed a stunning header into the top corner of the net.

Grays went close to re-instating their two goal lead a minute after but Brown denied Martin and with nine minutes remaining The Bulls levelled things up. Jeannin was again the provider, this time from a corner on the right, and it was Beckwith who met it with another good header that flew beyond the reach of Bayes. Purdie almost set up Andy Williams for a winner, when Williams turned his man in the box but saw his quick-fire effort saved by Bayes while a goalmouth scramble in injury time almost handed the match to the hosts, but Brown held onto the ball well.

All in all, it was a good result for Hereford having been 2-0 down at half time. A draw would probably have been deemed a good result at the start of the day and so it was quite pleasing in the end. The second half performance was again delightful from United, but the first half showing may not have been as pleasing. The severe lack of chances is something that must be looked at. However, if United can put in two "second half" performances against Cambridge on Tuesday, then they have a chance of moving into second place in the league.

HUFC: Brown, Travis, Mkandawire, Beckwith, Jeannin, Nicolau, Purdie, Ferrell, Williams, Stansfield, Ipoua. Subs: James, Mawson, Green, Stanley, Carey-Bertram.

GAFC: Bayes, Sambrook, Edwards, Hanson, Johnson, Kightly, Hooper, Thurgood, Martin, Battersby, McLean. Subs: Eyre, Nutter, Mawer, Slabber, Oli.

Williams fires United into top three

Hereford United moved into third place in the Nationwide Conference with a 3-0 home victory against Cambridge United this evening. The three points takes them into third place, but they are level on points with Exeter who occupy second. United's only change to the side that started against Grays was in attack, where Danny Carey-Bertram replaced the injured Guy Ipoua. Andy Williams played alongside Adam Stansfield though, and Carey-Bertram was on the right-wing.

The opening was a scrappy one, in which both sides enjoyed spells of possession without threatening a lot, although The U's almost took a stunning lead through ex-Bull Jon Brady. The Australian struck the cross bar with a delightful strike from twenty five yards that had beaten Wayne Brown in the Hereford goal. Courtney Pitt had the ball in the net for the visitors but was clearly offside when he headed in while, for Hereford, Carey-Bertram struck a cross from Nicky Nicolau wide at the far post.

It wasn't until thirty four minutes that United got a strike on goal, but it was well worth the wait for Stansfield's effort. He collected the ball some forty yards out, went on to take on three defenders before firing an unstoppable drive into the far top corner from the edge of the box for the opening goal. Stansfield again went close minutes later when he tackled the last man, Tommy Jaszczun, but chipped over. United furthered their lead before the break with another brilliant goal, this time from Stansfield's strike partner Williams. He collected a pass from Rob Purdie with his back to goal, span off his marker and hit a wonderful snap-shot that flew into the back of the net off the crossbar, with three minutes of the half remaining.

Cambridge came out for the restart full of fight and ready to attempt a comeback, but any hopes of theirs were dashed by man of the match Williams just five minutes into the half. United cleared their lines following a cross into the box and fed Stansfield down

Hereford United v Cambridge United

GOAL... Hereford striker Adam Stansfield puts the Bulls one up watched by Cambridge midfielders Tom Jaszczun and Jon Brady.

Hereford United v Cambridge United
Hereford United's new signing Stuart Fleetwood lays off a pass despite the challenge of Cambridge defender Andy Duncan.

Hereford United v Cambridge United
Hereford midfielder Andrew Ferrell challenges former team mate Jon Brady.

the right where he had acres of space to run into before picking out the run of Williams towards the far post. Williams stormed in and finished perfectly with his first touch to put the result beyond any doubt. Rob Newman introduced Fola Onibuje in to his attack, hoping that his height would help The U's salvage something from the game.

The aerial threat was Cambridge's only real danger but Brown didn't have to stretch

Hereford United v Cambridge United
Hereford striker Andrew Williams celebrates his spectacular goal watched by team mate Rob Purdie but Cambridge United midfielder David Bridges looks less than impressed.

to make a save all game. Mark Peters headed straight at him as he met a corner unchallenged while at the other end Williams went close to completing his hat trick before the hour mark. He dispossessed a defender but shot over the bar from twenty yards out. Purdie also missed the target from a similar range following a cleared free kick before Onibuje headed Brady's cross straight at Brown. And with twenty minutes left, Graham Turner introduced his new signing to the home crowd of 2,142 (including 84 away fans). Stuart Fleetwood replaced the hard-working Stansfield in attack.

The Welsh Under 21 international was straight into the action and forced his way through the U's defence and cut back into the centre where Williams cleverly let the ball run for Nicolau, and the loanee hit the foot of the post from eight yards. The visitors came closest to netting when they broke quickly, picking out Pitt, who'd split off to the left, but his cross was flashed wide of the far post by the head of Onibuje. Fleetwood, who showed some nice touches as well as pace and strength, blazed over from the edge of the box as the game came to a close.

So it finished 3-0 to The Whites and moves them up the league table, right into the thick of the play-offs. Other than the first twenty minutes, Hereford generally dominated and were rarely threatened by Cambridge and there was some nice football on show, especially in the second half when gaps appeared in the visitors defence as they went in search of some sort of consolation. Purdie again looked happier in his centre midfield role and the team seemed to again have added balance, presumably due to the addition of a left winger in Nicolau who played well. Maybe it is no coincidence that since Purdie has moved into the middle, The Bulls have scored 5 goals in two games. Goal scoring has been the department that they have struggled in for most of the season.

HUFC: Brown, Travis, Mkandawire, Beckwith, Jeannin, Carey-Bertram, Purdie, Ferrell, Nicolau, Williams, Stansfield. Subs: Mawson, James, Green, Stanley, Fleetwood.

CUFC: Howie, Morrison, Duncan, Peters, Jaszczun, Brady, Smith, Gleeson, Bridges, Pitt, Westcarr. Subs: Davies, Porter, Robinson, Heeroo, Onibuje

Hereford United v Grays Athletic, 4 February 2006. Report by Brian Goodwin

Holders tighten grip on Trophy

Grays Athletic overcame an, on the day, poor Hereford side to tighten their grip as holders on the F.A. Trophy at Edgar Street this afternoon.

Both sides made several changes from their previous outings, with United making six in total in just their starting eleven. Craig Mawson, Tony James, Ryan Green, Daryl Taylor, Craig Stanley and Stuart Fleetwood all started as Wayne Brown, Simon Travis, Dean Beckwith, Andy Ferrell, Danny Carey-Bertram and Adam Stansfield made way.

Hereford United v Grays FA Trophy.
Hereford United's Ryan Green runs at Grays defender Jamie Stuart.

Hereford United v Grays FA Trophy.
Grays goalkeeper Ashley Bayes tips away a Hereford attack.

Hereford enjoyed the majority of possession in the opening periods but it was the visitors who had the early chances. Aaron McLean got a run through on goal when Alex Jeannin miss controlled but was denied by Mawson and it was then the ever-impressive skipper Stuart Thurgood who worked some space, got a clear sight on goal in the box, but saw his shot rebound off the legs of Mawson.

Fleetwood burst through the Grays back line and forced a save from Ashley Bayes, despite the angle being very much against the striker and Bayes then gifted The Bulls another chances with a poor clearance, that led to Green having a shot deflected wide for a corner. Stanley almost scored a wonder-goal when he played a one-two with Andy Williams but his flying half-volley was just inches too high. James headed a Williams cross over just before the break as a pretty poor first half came to a close.

The second half wasn't any better either and, despite some neat passing from both sides, little in the way of goal scoring chances were created, until the hour mark when the headlock was broken. It was no surprise either that the goal came from a set-play, and was aided by a defensive lapse that allowed Michael Kightly to fire in, un-marked at the far post, to the the top corner on the half volley from Thurgood's corner.

Graham Turner rang the changes immediately with a triple substitution that saw Ferrell, Carey-Bertram and Stansfield replace Stanley, Taylor and Fleetwood respectively but to little effect. United continued to enjoy possession and a fair few crosses were delivered into the box, but it was

Hereford United v Grays FA Trophy.
Grays defender Jamie Stuart beats Hereford's Tamika Mkandawire in a heading duel.

Hereford United v Grays FA Trophy.
Hereford United's new signing Nicky Nicolau is beaten by Grays goalscorer Michael Kightly.

a Grays player who met them every time, other than when Williams glanced a header wide of the far post. With around five minutes remaining Carey-Bertram found space on the right flank and took the chance to run at the defence, who backed off. He shot powerfully but the ball hit the defender and rebounded to Stansfield. He, though, headed at goal when perhaps had the time to take a shot, and Bayes didn't have to move.

This was the final chance that United had of forcing a replay, which was probably the last thing they wanted. Six changes obviously disrupted the side and it will be no surprise to see just as many when Halifax visit Edgar Street next Saturday. No doubt both the players and the supporters, of which there were 1,609 (44 away) today, will be more "up" for the Conference fixture.

HUFC: Mawson, Green, James, Mkandawire, Jeannin, Nicolau, Purdie, Stanley, Taylor, Williams, Fleetwood. Subs: Beckwith, Ferrell, Caldicott, Carey-Bertram, Stansfield.

Hereford United v Halifax Town, 11 February 2006. Report by Kevin Goodwin

Stansfield snatches victory for the Bulls

Hereford United moved up to second in the table with a narrow win over their play-off rivals Halifax Town. Adam Stansfield was on hand to score the only goal of the game with twelve minutes remaining, latching on to a Craig Stanley back heel.

The Bulls made five changes from their FA Trophy defeat at the hands of Grays, Craig Mawson was replaced by Wayne Brown in between the sticks. Dean Beckwith returned for Tony James, Ryan Green came in at right back with Simon Travis moving to the bench.

Hereford United v Halifax Town
GOAL... Halifax defenders Steve Haslam, Adam Quinn and Steve Yates and goalkeeper Jon Kennedy can only look on as Hereford striker Adam Stansfield score the only goal of the game.

Rob Purdie failed to make the bench after he went down with a stomach bug, Andy Ferrell came in instead. Adam Stansfield was the final change made, coming in for Daryl Taylor who dropped to the bench, Andy Williams started on right midfield. John Grant returned to Edgar Street up top for Halifax.

Early on in the game, Halifax had an early chance to go in front after Matt Doughty shot from 25 yards forcing Brown into an early save. Hereford put on the pressure but failed to create any chances, until Stuart Fleetwood crossed in and Beckwith's volley was blocked. Alex Jeannin nearly opened the scoring when his free-kick took a deflection, but former Accrington Stanley shot stopper Jon Kennedy dived to his right and parried away for a corner.

Ferrell's persistence created a chance for Williams to cross in, Tamika Mkandawire met it with a side foot volley which went wide. The talking point of the first half came when Hereford had a strong appeal for a penalty, Fleetwood got into the box and tried to flick past the defender, the ball appeared to strike an arm but the ref and linesman waved play on. At the other end, Grant's run created an opening for Danny Forrest but his low drive was comfortably saved by Brown.

The second half started slowly for both sides. Halifax bought on Ryan Sugden for Brenton Leister. Grant hit a snapshot for the away side from around 30 yards but it was nearer the corner flag then it was to Brown's goal. Stansfield's run then created an opening for Nicky Nicolau, he took on the last defender but his final shot was weak and Kennedy saved. Steve Yates then came on for Greg Young as it seemed that Halifax were happy enough with a point.

Stansfield was once again involved as his dummy left Ferrell with a good shooting opportunity but he shot wildly over. Ferrell then shot over with his right foot after

Hereford United v Halifax Town

Former Hereford United forward Halifax John Grant uses his arm to control the ball while under pressure from Bulls defender Dean Beckwith.

Hereford United v Halifax Town

JUBILATION… For Hereford goalscorer Adam Stansfield as he celebrates the winner against Halifax with team mates.

Stansfield once again found him. Williams, who tired towards the end of the game, crossed in for Stansfield but his header was weak and straight at Kennedy. Beckwith burst out of defence and sent a long ball over the top, Stansfield once again was involved firing a low cross which Williams met, firing straight at the Kennedy's legs.

Unsurprisingly it was Stansfield who finally broke the deadlock with 78 minutes played.

Hereford United v Halifax Town

Hereford United's Nicky Nicolau evades the tackle from Halifax Town's Steve Haslam.

Stanley battled away to win the ball from a poor Doughty pass, and the ball fell to Fleetwood who crossed into the box. It looked as though it was an easy take for Kennedy but he spilt leaving Stanley, who had carried on with his run to collect, to direct a cheeky back-heel into the box and Stansfield was there to score his eighth of the season.

Halifax offered little threat when looking for the equaliser, Sugden's turn and shot was easily held by Brown. Taylor, who looked lively after replacing Nicolau, went on a mazy run before firing over from thirty yards. Simon Travis replaced Fleetwood, with Williams moving up front and Craig Midgley took the place of Halifax skipper Martin Foster.

Taylor once again ran down the left side leaving defenders behind with his pace before sending Stansfield through but his shot from a tight angle went narrowly wide of the far post. In stoppage time, Hereford had more chances to get a second, Green sent a long ball over the Halifax defence and Williams ran onto it before shooting low into the side netting. Stanley then found Travis on the burst into the box but the sub's drive was blocked.

It was a thoroughly entertaining game at Edgar Street this afternoon with Hereford deserving the three points. Halifax played their part in the game, with some neat attacking football but The Bulls had the edge in the end. Everyone in the side played their part in a decent team effort, with man of the match Jeannin just one player who stood out in front of a crowd of 2555 with 121 fans making the journey from Halifax.

HUFC: Brown, Green, Mkandawire, Beckwith, Jeannin, Williams, Ferrell, Stanley, Nicolau, Fleetwood, Stansfield. Subs: Mawson, Gwynne, Carey-Bertram, Travis, Taylor.

HTFC: Kennedy, Haslam, Quinn, Young , Doughty, Leister, Thompson, Foster, Killeen, Forrest, Grant. Subs: Bushell, Bowler, Yates, Sugden, Midgley.

Kington Town v Hereford United, 14 February 2006. Report by Kevin

Bulls cruise into local final

Hereford United put seven past local side Kington Town in a one sided encounter at Park Road this evening in front of around 250 supporters. A strong eleven was put out by Graham Turner including youngster Sam Gwynne as captain. Craig Mawson started in goal, Alex Jeannin played in an unfamiliar place in the middle of defence and Rob Purdie returned after illness. Stuart Fleetwood partnered Andy Williams up front.

Kington Town v Hereford United
Herefordshire Senior Cup
Girolami gets a grip of Andy Williams. Adriano is Hereford United's Football in The Community Officer.

United made a lively start to the game with Gwynne looking dangerous, he fired a decent drive forcing Kington 'keeper Kirkham to tip over. From the resulting corner, The Bulls took the lead. Dean Beckwith collected in the box and passed to Williams, who, from 8 yards, shot past the helpless Kirkham. Good work down the right from Daryl Taylor nearly resulted in a second for Hereford when Stanley connected well on the volley from the cross but Kirkham was equal to it.

Fleetwood's low shot from 20 yards was easily held by Kirkham but United were looking more and more like getting a second as the half progressed. Gwynne played a neat ball through the home side's defence and Fleetwood once again managed to get a shot in, this time it caused the 'keeper more concern but again he pulled of a decent save. Hereford finally made it two just minutes after; Williams did well to play in Fleetwood and his left foot shot gave the 'keeper no chance, scoring for the first time for Hereford.

Shortly after Rob Purdie's pace was too much for the Kington defence to handle as he ran into the box and was bought down. Simon Travis stepped up as the unlikely penalty taker, but he confidently dispatched it into the

Kington Town v Hereford United
Herefordshire Senior Cup

Hereford United youngster Sam Gwynne, who was captain for the game, is challenged by Kington Town's Russell Jones

corner giving Hereford a three goal advantage. Jeannin had a free kick tipped over by Kirkham and the 'keeper denied Fleetwood a second when his curling effort was parried out, but United had a strong appeal for a penalty at the end of the first half. Williams ran past the defender and was blatantly bought down, yet the referee failed to award a penalty, probably because of the earlier decision to award one.

Turner kept with the same eleven to start the second half, deciding against resting any first team players for the trip to Canvey. Fleetwood searched for a second as he took on the Kington defence, but after beating the 'keeper his touch was heavy and he couldn't direct the ball into the back of the net. A quick corner gave Fleetwood the opportunity to curl a shot but it narrowly missed the far top corner.

Stansfield came on for Jeannin and took up a role in central defence, and youngster Adam Worton replaced Purdie. Kington failed to test Mawson throughout the game, but their number 9 went close with a long range effort. Stanley raced on to a Fleetwood through ball, and was bought down by the 'keeper and the ref had no option but to give the second penalty of the game. Up stepped Fleetwood, who made no mistake, blasting home for his second of the evening.

Another youngster Kane Kahaki replaced Andy Williams, with Stansfield switching back to his preferred role up front. Gwynne picked up a booking for a late challenge which some supporters thought was harsh. The Bulls then took full advantage of a tiring Kington side, Ryan Green linked up well with Daryl Taylor down the right before delivering a inch perfect cross for Stansfield, who bagged his first of the evening. Yet it was Stansfield's strike partner, Fleetwood who made the biggest impression by gaining his hat trick. He curled a free-kick past the helpless Kirkham to make it six.

Stansfield then missed a simple chance after Stanley's toe poke had been blocked. Stansfield fired the rebound over the bar when it looked easier to score, but it was Stansfield who completed the rout by making it seven, running down the left hand side of the box before firing home from 15 yards.

Hereford won the game with ease, as they were expected despite the difficult playing conditions. Fleetwood will be pleased that he is off the mark with his hat trick, and Gwynne impressed in his midfield role. Youngsters Worton and Kahaki got their first ever senior games, but praise must all be given to Kington goalie Kirkham who made a string of good saves throughout the game to keep the score at just seven.

HUFC: Mawson, Green, Travis, Beckwith, Jeannin, Taylor, Gwynne, Stanley, Purdie, Williams, Fleetwood. Subs: Lewis, Stansfield, Ferrell, Kahaki, Worton.

Goals, a penalty, an injury, a red card, and three sets of fans

Hereford United dropped two vital points away at lowly Canvey Island this afternoon, but it was not just the loss of the points which will worry manager Graham Turner. The game was marred by a challenge on Adam Stansfield, that left him with a suspected fractured cheekbone. Also, the dismissal of Alex Jeannin in the second half could, in theory, lead to a five match ban.

The game took a while to produce a first effort on goal but it was the hosts who provided it, although John Keeling's half volley didn't trouble. Stansfield was first to threaten for The Bulls when he latched onto Jeannin's ball in behind the defence, but the strikers effort was turned behind by a recovering centre half. However, United managed to get their noses in front soon after, and it was Stansfield's strike partner Stuart Fleetwood who broke the deadlock. Following a surging run from the ex-Cardiff City forward, he played a neat one-two with Stansfield and then placed the ball low into the back of the net, although it was helped on its way by the goalpost.

The lead was short lived though, and three minutes later The Gulls found an equaliser. Kezie Ibe had got goal side of Tamika Mkandawire, and the Bulls skipper tugged him to the ground resulting in a penalty kick for the hosts. Neil Gregory made no mistake from the spot, sending Wayne Brown the wrong way. The shock injury, inflicted by John Kennedy, meant that Rob Purdie replaced Stansfield with five normal minutes of the half remaining in which time Jeannin saw a low drive saved, Nicky Nicolau's shot needed to be tipped round the post by Richard McKinney and at the other end Brown denied Mario Noto's free kick.

United had the better of the opening exchanges in the second period, but failed to force McKinney into a save, although Andy Ferrell, instrumental throughout, was just put off enough by a defender to stop him from meeting a perfect cross from Fleetwood. Then, with eleven minutes gone of the half, Jeannin received his marching orders in rather unclear circumstances. He was firstly booked, it is assumed, for a foul, which seemed a fair enough challenge, and then was shown a straight red card for, it is thought, foul and abusive language.

Canvey now had, understandably, renewed optimism and Noto became more and more dangerous for them. Brown had to pull off a great save to deny Noto almost immediately after the dismissal before United had the ball in the net for a second time. Craig Stanley sparked a counter attack, laying the ball into Andy Williams. He was held up by a defender but slipped the ball into Fleetwood who had the simple task of tucking the ball away beyond the reach of McKinney. However, the linesman on the far side adjudged Fleetwood to be offside and the goal did not count.

Nicolau was sacrificed as Simon Travis came on to play at left back but he gifted Noto a golden opportunity with a first, misjudged touch but luckily Noto's shot was wide. Ibe had two good chances on the turn in quick succession, the first being superbly tipped away by Brown and the second being smashed over the bar, both from close range. Fleetwood, who took a knock from 'keeper McKinney was replaced by Daryl Taylor with eighteen minutes to go, and Williams took up the lone role in attack. Mkandawire almost made amends for giving away the penalty when he fired just wide on the turn, following Purdie's delivery while Stanley also saw a shot saved as United pushed for the winner.

And it almost came right at the death, in the three minutes of injury time. Stanley's corner from the right fell to Dean Beckwith at the far post, who smashed a half volley in from little more than five yards out, but somehow McKinney got a hand to it and diverted it over the crossbar. Still though, there was another chance for the Bulls through Andy Ferrell. In the final moments he worked himself some space twenty odd yards from goal, unleashed a powerful low effort that seemed destined for the bottom corner, but again, somehow, McKinney got his outstretched fingertips to the ball and managed to, just, turn it around the post.

So it ended a goal apiece, thanks to some stern and, at times, desperate defending by the hosts, a penalty kick, a bad injury, a sending off, and some very dubious decisions by the one linesman. The result though, pleased the majority of the crowd of 784, of which around 200 were Hereford, a very few, apparently, were Accrington Stanley, and the rest were Canvey Island fans.

HUFC: Brown, Green, Mkandawire, Beckwith, Jeannin, Williams, Ferrell, Stanley, Nicolau, Stansfield, Fleetwood. Subs: Travis, Mawson, Purdie, Taylor, Gwynne.

CIFC: McKinney, Chenery, Ward, McGhee, Duffy, Noto, Kennedy, Sedgemore, Keeling, Ibe, Gregory. Subs: Potter, Dolan, Tait, Clarke, Minton.

Hereford United v Aldershot Town, 21 February 2006. Report by Brian Goodwin

Youngsters do the double for United

A first half double from the youthful front pairing of Andy Williams and Stuart Fleetwood was enough for Hereford United to complete their, now traditional, seasonal double over Aldershot Town. The United starting eleven held two changes from the one that started against Canvey Island on Saturday, with the suspended Alex Jeannin being replaced by Simon Travis and Daryl Taylor deputising for Adam Stansfield, with Williams moving into the attack. Matt Halliday was named on the bench.

Hereford United v Aldershot.
Hereford forward Andy Williams fires past Aldershot 'keeper Nikki Bull to put The Bulls 1-0 up.

United were ahead within three minutes, a whole extra minute than it took for them to take the lead at The Rec last September. Fleetwood was the producer, as he played the ball into space and left the Shots' defence for dead, before crossing for Williams, who made no mistake with a shot into the roof of the net. Hereford had set a tone for the rest of the half with this opening, and could have doubled the lead minutes later. Nicky Nicolau

Hereford United v Aldershot.
Hereford forward Andy Williams fires past Aldershot 'keeper Nikki Bull to put The Bulls 1-0 up.

found space on the left and crossed to the far post where both Craig Stanley and Taylor awaited. It was the latter who met the ball, but skied embarrassingly when unmarked.

Aldershot didn't force a save out of Wayne Brown until after the restart but Tamika Mkandawire needed to be alert to head a dangerous cross, that was flicked on, by Ryan Williams behind for a corner. United though, were again threatening following a good break down the right that saw Taylor's cross fall to Andy Williams, but he fired wide of the far post. However, it was not long before The Bulls found the net again and Fleetwood was again the main man involved.

Travis took a throw in on the left and Fleetwood held off Greg Heald and ran clear into the box. Nicki Bull came out to meet him but Fleetwood kept his composure and slotted into the back of the net with just under half an hour on the clock. Fleetwood and Williams were again linking up well but this time Williams' awesome shot from twenty five yards was tipped over the bar by Bull. The half came to a close following four successive corners for Hereford. Mkandawire came close on the third, forcing a good low save from Bull after Fleetwood had crossed and Dean Beckwith headed just wide on the final corner, which was delivered by Nicolau.

The second half though, was not as easy going for United as Aldershot began to gamble more men forward and gradually took control of the midfield area which Andy Ferrell had mastered so well in the first period. The goal though, on the hour mark, came some-what out of nothing, as United seemed to be under no real threat with the Meadow End in full voice behind them.

Hereford United v Aldershot.
Hereford's Daryl Taylor flicks a pass on while challenged by Aldershot's Darren Barnard.

Hereford United v Aldershot.
Aldershot 'keeper Nikki Bull punches clear just before Hereford striker Stuart Fleetwood.

Ryan Williams had crossed too far, but Hassan Sulaiman collected on the bye line. He was given too much time to pick out Gary Holloway who headed, unopposed, into the back of the net from close range for 2-1. Graham Turner reacted by bringing on Rob Purdie for Daryl Taylor, who'd been quite anonymous in the second half and Purdie was quick to contribute with some decent set-piece deliveries. It was his corner that almost led to a third goal for Hereford, but Mkandawire's header rebounded off the crossbar before Stanley saw a long range effort well held by Bull.

Fleetwood and Williams were again causing problems for the visitors defence as the former found the latter with a ball from the right, and Williams took a touch as his marker took a tumble, but Williams' early effort, when now one on one, was dragged wide of the mark. The latter stages of the game saw Aldershot really push for the equaliser, setting up a nervy finish for the hosts. Holloway had ambitiously hooked over with a bicycle kick in the 89th minutes, but the real scare came in the third and final minute of injury time. After gaining possession back off Hereford, who'd run time down in the corner, Aldershot raced forward and found themselves with three attackers against two defenders. Ryan Williams found Leroy Griffiths with a through-ball, but Brown was quickly out and blocked the shot.

So United held on for the vital three points that takes them back into second place in the Conference. It has to be said that man of the match Fleetwood and Andy Williams linked up very well and luckily the absence of Adam Stansfield did not have as much of an effect on the team as his return from injury had earlier in the season. The crowd of 2,205, including 127 away fans, made for a very good atmosphere at Edgar Street and hopefully the Sky TV camera's will not affect the attendance too much next Monday, when Stevenage Borough are the visitors.

HUFC: Brown, Green, Beckwith, Mkandawire, Travis, Nicolau, Ferrell, Stanley, Taylor, Fleetwood, Williams. Subs: Halliday, Mawson, Gwynne, Purdie, Carey-Bertram.

ATFC: Bull, Hamilton, Brough, Heald, Barnard, Sulaiman, Somner, Holloway, Williams, Dixon, Griffiths. Subs: Weait, Elphick, Hudson, Jinadu, Salmon.

Hereford United v Stevenage Borough, 27 February 2006. Report by Brian Goodwin

Willo in Wonderland

Andy Williams was in dream land once again as he found the score sheet for the second game in a row, moving his season total up to eleven goals of which seven have come in the Nationwide Conference. The youngster again impressed this evening, in front of a wider audience than usual with the game being live on Sky, as Hereford United defeated play off rivals Stevenage Borough at Edgar Street.

United, who were unchanged from the side that started last week against Aldershot, started well but failed to really test Alan Julian in the Boro goal in the early stages. Stuart Fleetwood, who is also making quite a name for himself at Edgar Street, had a shot blocked in the opening stages and then moments later Stevenage threatened for the first time when Dino Maamria volleyed wide at the near post.

Tamika Mkandawire's header, from Ryan Green's free kick was saved by Julian before

Hereford United v Stevenage Borough

Hereford United winger Daryl Taylor is impeded by Stevenage Borough's Justin Gregor watched by the Borough bench. Gregory was sent off for the challenge after receiving the second yellow card of the game.

Nicky Nicolau was replaced, on seventeen minutes, by Rob Purdie due to injury. Williams latched onto a flick-header by Fleetwood but a defender was in the way of his shot while, at the other end, George Boyd almost created a goal out of nothing. He caught the ball on the full volley twenty five yards from goal, almost catching Wayne Brown out, but the 'keeper managed to scramble across his line to push the ball behind.

Fleetwood and Andy Ferrell both had shots saved before the deadlock was broken in the final minute of first half added time. Ferrell delivered a free kick into the box, which was met by the head of Dean Beckwith and Williams was on hand in the middle to stretch out a leg and volley high into the net from around eight yards.

Boyd again forced Brown into a brilliant save just after the restart as the goalie clawed an effort from the winger out of the air extravagantly but it was the Bulls who were to score again and put a clear margin between the two sides. Green took a throw in on the right which Williams touched to Craig Stanley. Stanley played another short ball to Fleetwood who, with his back to goal, span off his marker before planting a shot across the helpless Julian and into the far bottom corner.

Jefferson Louis, one of three first half bookings for the more-than-physical side, almost grabbed one back for the visitors a minute later but saw his curling effort rebound back into play off the post and from then on United were in complete control. Mkandawire headed just over from a Ferrell, impressive again in midfield, free kick crossed to the far

Hereford United v Stevenage Borough
Hereford United's defender Tamika Mkandawire heads just over the Stevenage goal.

post before Fleetwood showed he is human after all when he fired wide of the mark, having skinned two opponents.

Then, rather inevitably, a red card was produced for a Stevenage player with twenty minutes left on the clock. Justin Gregory, who had been terrorised by the pace of Daryl Taylor all evening had already picked up a first half booking and left the referee, Rob Lewis, no choice but to show him a second when he tripped Taylor as the winger skipped past him once again. Ronnie Henry had to be careful to clear over his cross bar as he got a foot to an inviting Taylor cross from the right with attackers lurking at the far post. Then, from the resulting corner, more danger lingered for Boro. Fleetwood crossed to outside of the box where man of the match Stanley awaited before unleashing a thunderous volley that flew just inches over the bar.

Julian showed good hands to deny Williams a second goal, as the attacker beat his man from the bye line, leaving Henry to head behind before Danny Carey-Bertram was given two minutes (and the four injury time minutes) to have a run out, in the place of Taylor and then seventeen year-old Sam Gwynne was given his debut in place of Fleetwood.

There were some very impressive individual performances this evening, but everyone worked well together also and, in the end, United quite easily overcame what appeared to be a very difficult fixture. In particular Beckwith, Stanley, Ferrell, Williams and Fleetwood stood out. The result takes United back into second place and leave Stevenage where they were before in fourth position. The only slightly disappointment of the evening was the attendance, no doubt affected by the live coverage on Sky, which was 2,394 including 41 away fans.

Hereford v Stevenage Borough

CHARGING BULL... Hereford striker Stuart Fleetwood rushes towards the home fans after scoring United's second against Stevenage.

Hereford United v Stevenage Borough

Hereford players celebrates Stuart Fleetwood second against Stevenage.

HUFC: Brown, Green, Mkandawire, Beckwith, Travis, Nicolau, Ferrell, Stanley, Taylor, Williams, Fleetwood. Subs: Haliday, Mawson, Purdie, Gwynne, Carey-Bertram.

SBFC: Julian, Hocking, Quinn, Henry, Gregory, Bulman, Berquez, Miller, Boyd, Maamria, Louis. Subs: Goodliffe, Weatherstone, Obinna, Nurse, Stamp.

Gravesend & Northfleet v Hereford United, 7 March 2006 by Ex Landlord

Fleet Sunk By Teenage Torpedos

On the 31st of August 1946 the then fledgling Gravesend and Northfleet played their first game in the old Southern League. They represented an amalgamation Gravesend United and Northfleet United and their opponents on that day were none other than Hereford United. The Fleet ran out 3-0 victors on the day in front of over 5000 spectators who each paid one shilling and three pence (6p today) to watch the match. Last night a gate of just 618 including around 100 travelling Bulls fans who each paid £12 to stand on an uncovered terrace in wind and rain watched United rally from a goal down to win 2-1 and return home with three valuable points.

Second half goals from newcomer Robbie King and the ever-improving Andy Williams turned an apparent lost cause into a memorable victory.

Bulls boss Graham Turner again had to juggle his injury and suspension hit squad moving the versatile Rob Purdie to yet another unfamiliar role at left back and bringing in Colchester's nineteen-year-old academy player Robbie King for his debut in a Bulls shirt. Bulls lined up with Wayne Brown in goal and a back four of Green, Tammy, Beckwith and Purdie. The midfield comprised of Taylor, Stanley, Ferrell and King with Fleetwood and Williams up front.

Early in the game Green supplied Williams with an opportunity to break into the box but the young strikers low cross was cleared by McCarthey before a Ferrell corner was cleared to Stanley who laid the ball to Rob Purdie to shoot just wide of the upright. A free kick for the hosts 35 yards from goal was taken by Johnson and played wide right to the overlapping Gooding who blazed high, wide and not so handsome. On the ten minute mark, a long ball found Andy Williams on the edge of the box and his neat flick fell to the advancing Craig Stanley who squeezed his effort a foot wide. Two minutes later, Rawle jinked passed Ryan Green and sprinted at the United goal but Brown was swiftly out to narrow angle and force the Fleet striker to shoot wide.

There then followed a 15 minute period of particularly scrappy play when Hereford looked to be struggling to come to terms with their task and seemed short on confidence although at no time did the effort fall short. Daryl Taylor had been on the receiving end of a couple late tackles before he found himself dispossessed near the halfway line by Johnson. The Walsall loanee challenged as the loose ball bounced up and caught Johnson at what appeared to be knee height while going for the ball. From the far side of the pitch, the challenge did not look bad but the referee produced a red card and Taylor had to leave the field. Fleet assumed control and took the lead on 32 minutes when Gooding, again advancing from his full back role delivered a pin-point far post cross for the unmarked Jimmy Jackson to head in off the post. Six minutes later Jackson, again unmarked, should have doubled the lead when presented with a golden opportunity but he blasted over the bar from 15 yards out.

As the half time whistle blew it was not easy to see how the ten shell-shocked men of Hereford could stage a come back.

As the second half progressed the Bulls slowly but surely clawed their way back into the game and only a desperate challenge by McCarthey after nine minutes of the half prevented Andy Williams bursting through on goal – a yellow card was produced as a result. Shortly after, Fleetwood laid the ball back to Stanley who threaded a delightful ball through to Williams for the youngster to flick into the path of Andy Ferrell who was steaming into the box. Ferrell and the well-built McCarthey met the ball at the same time but it was the Fleet defender who came off worse and he had to leave the field to be replaced with Fuller. Purdie was by now playing in a more forward role and he delivered a superb cross which Mkandawire headed just over despite being clattered by the advancing 'keeper. United continued to press with Fleetwood and Williams both looking dangerous. Williams was playing a central role while Fleetwood worked tirelessly off the ball to create space and was rewarded by a thumping tackle from behind which earned a booking for Jackson on 72 minutes. Then, two minutes later came the breakthrough. Ferrell floated a free kick into the box, which was headed clear, but the ball landed at the feet of Robbie King who took one touch before flashing the ball through a narrow gap and into the net.

Just 5 minutes later, United took the lead with another fine goal. Ryan Green found Williams 40 yards from goal and despite being surrounded by three defenders the local boy dragged the ball back and spun passed them before sprinting forward to unleash an unstoppable low shot from just inside the box which scorched into the net.

Late in the game, Fleet threw on an extra attacker in the shape of Sodje but it was the Bulls who finished in control although both Fleetwood and Williams looked exhausted by their efforts at the end.

For the second time this season Hereford had come from behind to win with ten men away from home and as before, when Ipoua was dismissed at Exeter, there may be cause to look at the video evidence surrounding a red card incident!

Gravesend: Holloway, Gooding, Smith R., McCarthey, Watkins, Slatter, McKimm, Johnson, Jackson, Moore, Rawle. Subs: Kerr, Smith J., Fullar, Sodje, Saunders

Hereford: Brown, Green, Mkandawire, Beckwith, Purdie, Taylor, Stanley, King, Ferrell, Williams, Fleetwood. Subs: Mawson, James, Gwynne, Carey-Bertram, Holliday

Man of the Match: Dean Beckwith

Rule Bulltania
Ex-Landlord

Hereford United v Accrington Stanley, 11 March 2006. Report by Brian Goodwin

"Come-back Kings" do it again!

Hereford United are making a name for themselves with their impressive come-backs and today fought back from 2-0 down against run-away League leaders Accrington Stanley, who came to Edgar Street boasting a ten game winning streak. A win for the Lancashire side would have equalled Hereford United's Conference Record of eleven games won in a row.

One forced change was made from the trip to Gravesend and Northfleet, with the suspended Daryl Taylor beginning a three match ban. In came Nicky Nicolau, back from injury on the left wing and Robbie King played on the opposite flank. And despite United's youthful, injury hit side, they had the better of the opening stages against the Champions elect. Andy Ferrell, back in the centre of midfield alongside Craig Stanley, won a corner off his early free kick, which deflected off the wall before King had a good opening. Andy Williams broke on the right, pulled the ball back into the box where King arrived, only to blaze over from twelve yards. King then turned provider for Williams, but the latter's header was easily saved.

Accrington reacted well though and began to venture forwards more often, pushing the Bulls onto the back foot. Stanley, who'd been breaking up Accy attacks well in the midfield,

Hereford United v Accrington Stanley.
GOAL... Hereford's Nicky Nicolau hits the equaliser against Accrington Stanley watched by defender Ryan Green.

Hereford United v Accrington Stanley.
HAND BALL... Accrington Stanley defender Danny Ventre clearly handles the ball.
Although the penalty was saved striker Stuart Fleetwood scored the off the rebound.

was back quickly to put a dangerous Todd cross behind for a corner, which was taken short to Ian Craney and then to Romauld Bobo, whose effort was deflected just wide of the post. The dangerous Gary Roberts shot over following the second corner kick, and he was again off target minutes later, but the visitors had the lead with thirty seven minutes on the clock. And to add insult to injury it was, almost inevitably, the only former Hereford player on the pitch, David Brown, who netted. Brown stood with his back to goal at a tight angle, as a throw in was taken. It bounced up nicely for him and he hooked the ball over his shoulder, over the head of Wayne Brown, and into the far side of the net for 1-0.

United reacted positively though, and Stuart Fleetwood's powerful run found its way to Williams, who saw his shot go wide having taken a touch off a defender and minutes before the break Williams had the ball in the back of the net. Stanley delivered a free kick, which 'keeper Rob Elliot came to claim but let loose, and Williams was quickly on hand to turn the ball into the back of the net. However, referee M Mullarkey saw a foul on Elliot and ruled the goal out, and so the league leaders went in at the break a goal to the good.

Craney opened the second half with a booking, which set the tone for the next ten to fifteen minutes or so – the game became scrappy and neither side really threatened each others goal. It was Craig Stanley who managed to carve an opening though as he picked out yet another excellent pass into the run of King, who'd advanced into the penalty box. King beat his marker but was then taken down by the on rushing goalie Elliot, who

Hereford United v Accrington Stanley.
Hereford's Tamika Mkandawire challenges Accrington Stanley's Romauld Boco and Philip Edwards.

clattered the youngster to the ground and the ball bounced away. Williams gathered but shot against an opponent and out for a throw in, but the Hereford players and fans were incensed that Mr. Mullarkey had failed to give a penalty. Matters were then made worse for United as Accrington broke away, won a corner and, against the run of play, doubled their advantage.

Craney fiercely fired in the corner to the near post where the ball took a wicked deflection off skipper Tamika Mkandawire and flew into the back of the net, leaving Wayne Brown with no chance. The game was all but settled, as was the league title, and a reserved atmosphere filled Edgar Street. That was, however, until Ryan Green stepped up and burst out of defence. He flew forwards and was on the end of a one-two with King on the right and delivered a low cross into the box, which was missed by Williams but not by Nicolau who floated in at the far post, smashed in a goal bound effort that was cleared off the line by Danny Ventre. With his hand according to Mr Mullarkey. The red card was issued, Rob Purdie, filling in well at left back, stepped up but missed! Elliot flung himself to his left, got a hand to it, and pushed the ball against the bar and it fell back into play. Thankfully for Purdie, Fleetwood was the first man to react and he volleyed in from close range. Mayhem in the Meadow End, and it was game on.

The Bulls then ran riot, flying forward at every opportunity with even Mkandawire getting forward. Dean Beckwith thought he had equaliser when he towered high at the far post to meet a corner, but was to be denied by a man on the line. Williams was next on hand to go oh-so-close, when he got around his man on the edge of the box but saw his well hit low shot excellently pushed behind for a corner by Elliot, yet to lose with Accrington, and then Mkandawire headed just wide at the far post from another corner. Time was running out though and it almost seemed too little, too late when Ferrell was denied by another great stop. His low drive from twenty yards seemed destined for the bottom corner but an outstretched hand from Elliot diverted it just wide and then a boost was handed for all but the 283 Accrington fans in

Hereford United v Accrington Stanley.
GOAL... Hereford's Nicky Nicolau celebrates hitting the equaliser with Bulls fans.

a highest crowd of the season of 4,497 at Edgar Street. Six minutes of injury time, accumulated from the sending off, some time wasting by Accy players and non-playing staff. The Bulls took full advantage.

A fantastic passing move, triggered by man of the match Craig Stanley, found its way into the feet of Williams, who brilliantly flicked the ball over the defence and perfectly into the path of the run of Nicolau, who beat the advancing Elliot with a wonderful full volley in front of the Meadow End. The fans were delirious and wanted a third, but time ran out, thankfully for Accrington, who were crumbling fast.

It was not the result that United needed to really have any chance of catching Accrington, but all the same the side showed great character to fight back and gain a deserved draw against the sure to be future champions. After the first hour of play it looked as though it would definitely not be Hereford's day, but with the help of the crowd and a red card, it made for an extremely entertaining final half hour. Hereford now, though, need to follow up this result with a win against Southport on Tuesday evening as they hope to cut into Accrington's sixteen point lead.

HUFC: Brown, Green, Mkandawire, Beckwith, Purdie, Nicolau, Ferrell, Stanley, King, Fleetwood, Williams. Subs: James, Haliday, Mawson, Gwynne, Carey-Bertram.

ASFC: Elliot, Ventre, Welch, Edwards, Boco, Williams, Todd, Roberts, Craney, Mullin, Brown. Subs: Alcock, Boyd, Jagielka, Cook, Mangan.

Southport v Hereford United, 14 March 2006-. Report by Ex Landlord

Bulls hang on for three points

Hereford United secured another away victory in a hard fought game at Haig Avenue, Southport on a soft pitch which cut up quite badly as the match progressed.

Manager Graham Turner had to, again, shuffle his pack to bring in Tony James for the injured Dean Beckwith with Alex Jeannin also returning from suspension in place of Rob Purdie. The extent of Turner's depleted squad was emphasized by the fact that coach, John Trewick, was named amongst the substitutes. Southport kicked off facing the visiting Bulls fans but it was United who were quickly onto the attack with Jeannin robbing Morley on the halfway line before advancing down the wing and delivering a trademark centre which Williams glanced over.

The Bulls were in domination early on with a Green throw-in allowing Fleetwood to win a corner which was cleared up-field for Ports first meaningful attack on six minutes. It was, however, United that took the lead with just over nine minutes gone. The ball was played forward to Andy Williams who controlled it on his chest before feeding Fleetwood whose shot was cleared at the expense of a corner. Nicky Nicolau's cross was met by the downward header of Mkandawire for a classic finish. to give United a deserved 1-0 advantage.

Southport were forced into making an early substitution on 14 minutes when Carl Baker fell awkwardly and had to be replaced by Robbie Booth. Shortly afterwards Ferrell, who was clearly in the mood for some action, burst into the Port penalty area only to see his effort palmed away by the increasingly busy Steve Dickinson. The ball ran to Williams who turned it back across the goalmouth where King miss-directed his shot for a goal kick. Port did get the ball into the net on 20 minutes through Steve Daly but referee Richardson had already blown for offside. Three minutes later, the Bulls had Wayne

Brown to thank for a fine one handed save from Daly while falling backwards. Then a crisp four man move initiated by Craig Stanley which swept the length of the field finished with Ferrell, again in the box, seeing his shot deflected wide. On 42 minutes however Ferrell was rewarded for his graft. James played a ball out of defence to Stanley who made good ground down the right side before clipping an inch perfect ball into the box for the charging Andy Ferrell to power a header past Dickinson for United's second goal of the night. In first half stoppage time, ex Bull Chris Lane sent in a useful cross which Neil Robinson headed just wide.

HT – Southport 0 Hereford United 2

Southport Manager Liam Watson introduced both his remaining substitutes at the recommencement replacing Gary Brabin with Jerome Fitzgerald and Dominic Morley with Kevin Leadbetter.

The lively Stuart Fleetwood was soon in the thick of things again as he wriggled past three defenders before seeing the ball run away over the goal line. From the resulting goal kick, the ball spun off the foot of a Port defender to hit Andy Williams full in the face. The young striker had to leave the field for several minutes while the flow of blood from his nose was stemmed. On 51 minutes, Chris Lane, who was having an increasing influence, saw his effort rise just over Brown's crossbar. As play swung from end to end, Fleetwood again outpaced the Port defence only for the onrushing Dickinson to smother his effort. From the goalkeepers clearance came an attack down the flank which produced a deep cross into the Hereford penalty area and Mkandawire was adjudged to -have handed the ball as he attempted to head clear. Robinson stepped up to take the resulting penalty and blasted the ball passed Wayne Brown to put Southport back in the game on 59 minutes. Robinson also collected an entry in the referee's notebook for his over enthusiastic celebration.

Shortly afterwards, Andy Williams reluctantly left the field with a continuing nose bleed to be replaced by Danny Carey-Bertram. DCB was soon in action as Jeannin threaded a ball through for him chase into the box but his shot was blocked by Earl Davies. Port began to take control as Williams' ball winning and holding skills were missed. On 70 minutes, Daly and the Hereford 'keeper collided just inside the box and as Brown got to his feet he allegedly trod on the Port striker. There followed a "ruck" involving 8 or 10 players during which a punch was clearly thrown at Brown. As it calmed down, Leadbetter appeared to receive a yellow card. If this was for the punched, then he should consider himself extremely fortunate not to have left the field. Ferrell complained and was added to the list of cautions. When asked, after the match, Ferrell confirmed he had been booked by the referee who had apparently said, "well, I had to book someone"!

As the game became more fraught, Graham Turner took the sensible decision to replace Nicolau with "old hand" Jamie Pitman with 13 minutes left on the clock and he was soon in the action stepping in with some timely interceptions. Southport continued to pressure the United rearguard but it was Craig Stanley who almost produced a goal on 85 minutes when his deft chip from 25 yards landed on the roof of the net. The Bulls saw out the last few minutes with some fairly "rustic" defending – Ryan Green launching one particular clearance into row Z!

It was not the best of games and afterwards coach John Trewick described the performance as "sub-standard" and hinted that there had been signs in training that an "after the Lord Mayors Show" affect might have been on the cards following the Accrington game. He was, of course, more than happy to return to

Hereford with three points on the front seat of the team bus.

Southport – Dickinson, Lane, Powell. Brabin (Fitzgerald 45), Davis, Baker (Booth 14)Morley (Leadbetter 45), Blakeman, Pickford, Robinson, Daly. Subs not used – Speare, Fitzhenry

Hereford – Brown, Green, Mkandawire, James, Jeannin, King, Stanley, Ferrell, Nicolau (Pitman 88), Williams (Carey-Bertram 60), Fleetwood. Subs not used – Mawson, Gwynne, Trewick (Aged 48?)

Attendance 1057 (est. 120 HUFC)

HUFC Man of the Match – Andy "Mad Dog" Ferrell

Burton Albion v Hereford United, 18 March 2006. Report by Brian Goodwin

Hereford capitalise as Stanley draw

Hereford United cut into Accrington Stanley's lead at the top of the Nationwide Conference table this afternoon, as the run-away leaders dropped points against Stevenage Borough on home turf and Hereford capitalised by collecting all three points on their travels against Burton Albion at the Pirelli Stadium.

United, with Ryan Green added to the injury list from the game at Southport (meaning Rob Purdie filling in at left back and Dean Beckwith returning to the bench), took charge of the opening stages but had to wait until the quarter of an hour mark before even going close to scoring. Alex Jeannin dinked a ball into the box, where Tamika Mkandawire headed down for Stuart Fleetwood. The ball didn't drop kindly for the Welsh u21 international, but he still directed the ball onto the cross bar. Fleetwood again threatened, but this time fired wide of the far post, having received the ball from Andy Williams, who played a neat flick on.

Burton came into the game briefly, and went close after Craig Stanley had squandered possession deep inside his own half. The ball was spread to the left and cut back to Kris Taylor, but he scuffed his shot wide of the far post. Andy Ferrell, tenacious as ever in the middle, forced a low save from Saul Deeney, who gathered the powerful drive at the second attempt but he was beaten five minutes before the break. Alex Jeannin delivered a free kick into the box, which was headed down by Stanley to the feet of Williams. Williams scuffed his first effort and Deeney appeared to have collected, but the ball ran loose and Williams made no mistake the second time, firing high into the net from close range.

Wayne Brown had to be alert after the restart, as a resurgent Burton came out to attack United. Jon Shaw seemed certain to score from almost point-blank range, but somehow Brown dived across his goal to push the ball wide of his right-hand post. Skipper Darren Stride then had an even better opportunity as a ball in arrived from the left but somehow, from a central position about six yards out, he managed to fire a first time effort over the cross bar. Albion were piling on the pressure and it was some relief for the Bulls defence when Williams fired in a reminder at the other end, but Deeney made easy work of the twenty five yard effort. Taylor again went close for the Brewers, but again his effort was just wide of the far post while Gary Rowett went forced a goal mouth scramble with his downward header, following a corner, but the Bulls defence managed to scrap it clear.

With ten minutes left Fleetwood, who seemed a little off the pace, was replaced by Danny Carey-Bertram and, with United under almost constant pressure, Jamie Pitman replaced Nicky Nicolau with five minutes left. In those five minutes Burton, yet again, could have snatched what would have probably been a deserved equaliser and it was again the dangerous Taylor who went close. He was on the end of a whipped cross from the right with a diving header, but fortunately for Hereford, it was straight at Brown. A drive from the edge of the box took a deflection before going inches wide as the Brewers continued to push and in the last minute, after a throw in, Rowett turned the ball just wide again in what proved to be the last chance for the hosts.

Again without playing too well, like at Southport, United managed to overcome what proved to be a difficult fixture against an in-form side. With most results going for Hereford, this may prove to be a vital three points, and it sees them cement their place in second in the league, six points ahead of Halifax in third and ten points ahead of Stevenage who occupy the final play off spot.

HUFC: Brown, Purdie, James, Mkandawire, Jeannin, Nicolau, Stanley, Ferrell, King, Williams, Fleetwood. Subs: Beckwith, Mawson, Gwynne, Pitman, Carey-Bertram.

BAFC: Deeney, Corbett, Tinson, Rowett, Webster, Chris Hall, Stride, Kris Taylor, Gilroy, Shaw, Harrad. Subs: Henshaw, Austin, Martin Taylor, Ducros, Christian Moore.

Hereford United v Kidderminster Harriers, 25 March 2006. Report by Brian Goodwin

Derby Defeat

On a day when everything could have gone so well for Hereford United, it all went so badly. There were, undoubtedly, a couple of crucial points in the game where the balance was tipped towards the visitors, Kidderminster Harriers, firstly when Andy Ferrell was sent off and later on when Kiddy scored the only goal of the game, moments after Andy Williams had squandered a glorious chance to break the deadlock.

Hereford United v Kidderminster Harriers

SO CLOSE... Hereford captain Tamika Mkandawire's header is on its way to just missing the Kidderminster upright.

Hereford United v Kidderminster Harriers
Hereford captain Tamika Mkandawire covers his face after missing a chance against Kiddy.

United, who had Daryl Taylor and Ryan Green back in the starting eleven, with Adam Stansfield returning on the bench, started on the back foot and Tony James had to be aware to head a looping header off the line early on. Harriers continued to press forwards and it was Gareth Sheldon who forced Wayne Brown into a low save after a long free kick had fallen at his feet. Moments later Sheldon turned provider with a low cross from the right, but nobody met it as it slid across the goal face.

Stuart Fleetwood had United's first effort, and perhaps should have done better with it. Rob Purdie broke from inside the Hereford half before finding Williams. Williams played the ball onto his strike partner Fleetwood, who past his marker Jon Newby, before placing the ball just wide of the far post when he had just 'keeper John Danby to beat. Johnny Mullins was next to threaten for the visitors; his header from a free kick forced Brown into a wonderful save before Tamika Mkandawire almost netted at the other end, also after a free kick. Alex Jeannin crossed and the skipper stormed in at the near post only to see his bullet header fly inches wide of the near post.

Immediately, at the other end, Kiddy had another good chance, in what was an entertaining first half, when Paul Smith nutmegged Jeannin on his way through to goal, but drilled wide of the far post from the edge of the box. Then, when things seemed to be going well for United, with news (at this point in the game) of Accrington Stanley losing at York City, Ferrell was dismissed after reacting angrily to a nasty challenge from Terry Fleming, which left Ferrell with a gashed leg. Ferrell was straight back up after the initial foul scrapping for the ball at Fleming's feet, but the referee judged Ferrell to have aimed a stamp at Fleming. Ferrell received his marching orders while Fleming was booked, with ten minutes of the half remaining.

Johnny Harkness was then booked soon after, as he felled Daryl Taylor who'd beaten him for pace yet again before Luke Reynolds shot into the arms of Brown before the half time whistle was blown.

The game became scrappy after the restart and chances were few and far between. Daryl Burgess should have done better when he headed over a corner from a central position, but it took The Bulls around twenty minutes of the half to even get a shot away, as Jeannin blasted over a free kick from twenty five yards. Fleetwood, now playing on the left wing following Ferrell's red card, was replaced by Stansfield while Mark Yates, the Kiddy boss, withdrew Reynolds and sent on Lee Thompson. Stansfield almost made a difference with one of his first touches as he flicked a long ball from Jeannin onto Williams, who found himself free in the box, through on goal, with just Danby to beat. However, he couldn't compose himself and shot inches wide of the far post.

It was looking as though United wouldn't ever score, and matters were made worse as a moment later the deadlock was broken, in

Hereford United v Kidderminster Harriers.
OUCH... Kidderminster forward Luke Reynolds looks to be on the painful end of an encounter with Hereford's Ryan Green and Daryl Taylor.

Hereford United v Kidderminster Harriers.
Referee C Sarginson gives Hereford's Andy Ferrell the red card.

the seventy second minute. Michael Blackwood stormed down the middle of the park and found himself in some space thirty yards out. He cracked in a low shot that took a wicked deflection off Mkandawire, which totally wrong-footed Brown, and flew into the opposite corner that Brown had moved towards.

United didn't have a response to the goal, though they threw Jamie Pitman on to try and help the midfield, as Taylor was replaced. Reynolds forced Brown into another save, with a shot on the turn from the edge of the box, while Hereford's only chance of an equaliser came in injury time, when Pitman crossed to the near post for Williams, but his header was well over the bar.

News had already reached Edgar Street that Accy were 4-2 up at York by the full time whistle, leaving the Hereford fans in a crowd of 4,223, very dejected, while Kiddy fans (all 398 of them) were delirious at a rare win for their side, especially as it pretty much ends any slim title hopes that Bulls fans may have held before the game.

It's back to the drawing board for Hereford, as they put in a third successive poor performance. Maybe Dean Beckwith will return to the side, having missed the past three games, firstly through suspension and then as he couldn't regain his place – quite surprising as he has formed a very good partnership with Mkandawire.

HUFC: Brown, Green, James, Mkandawire, Jeannin, Purdie, Stanley, Ferrell, Taylor, Williams, Fleetwood. Subs: Beckwith, Mawson, Pitman, Nicolau, Stansfield.

KHFC: Danby, Harkness, Burgess, Newby, Mullins, Rea, Penn, Fleming, Blackwood, Sheldon, Reynolds. Subs: Lewis, Hurren, Sedgemore, Thompson, Russell.

Draw was on the Cards

Hereford United continued their quest to cement their place in the play offs with an away trip to Kingfield, home of Woking – who were hoping to creep into the end of season lottery themselves.

Just one change was made from the dismal home defeat last weekend, as Robbie King deputised for the suspended Andy Ferrell in the middle. The game began, but was bought to a stop for a few minutes almost immediately as Tony James was in need of the magic sponge, following a collision with Steve Ferguson, who gave James a torrid time throughout.

Craig Stanley came closest to giving the Bulls a first half lead with United's first major attack, following a good ball from Stuart Fleetwood to pick out the run of Rob Purdie towards the left flank. Purdie's delivery found Stanley storming through the middle, but his half volley, which hit the underside of the cross bar, was cleared away off the line. At the other end Wayne Brown almost made a hash up, as he came to the edge of the box to head away a high ball, but gifted it to Ferguson but the 'keeper managed to scramble in front of the attackers first effort, before the ball bounced back to him. James, though, was in the right place at the right time to clear the ball off the goal line.

Stephen Evans played a neat headed one-two with Craig McAllister, which found the former in a central position with plenty of space, but he rashly volleyed over from twelve yards out. James misjudged a long ball towards the Hereford back line to almost disastrous consequences, but luckily, when Ferguson stole in, he lifted the ball wide of the far post. King dragged an effort wide in a rare United effort at goal minutes before the break, but right on the stroke of half time the deadlock was broken. Ryan Green conceded a free kick almost right on the corner flag and Karl Murray's cross was perfect for McAllister to nod in unopposed, as Purdie had allowed him too much space, at the far post.

Graham Turner didn't make any changes at the break, but four minutes after the restart he did; James was replaced by Dean Beckwith and six minutes later Fleetwood made way for Adam Stansfield. United were dominant in the second half and had all the goal scoring opportunities, but didn't look likely to make the break-through. Daryl Taylor headed wide a cross from Alex Jeannin before Taylor had another effort, this time Andy Williams the provider, when he cut inside from the right and shot wide of the far post.

With eleven minutes left on the clock Jamie Pitman was introduced in place of King and The Bulls seemed to become more threatening again. A good succession of passes allowed the ball to find its way to Williams on the edge of the box, but his turn and shot was tipped away by the outstretched hand of Shwan Jalal. Jeannin lofted in a free kick as United pressed forward, but Stansfield shot into the arms of Jalal after Taylor had headed on but finally Hereford equalised with eighty nine minutes on the clock. Green took a throw in, which was returned by Taylor, and the Welsh man crossed right onto the head of the magnificent Tamika Mkandawire, who headed into the top right hand corner, much to the delight of the 300 or so away fans, in a crowd of 1,929.

A good point it turned out to be, in a game of two halves. United were more than deserving of their late equaliser, as they had swept the hosts aside in the second half. It was only a lapse of concentration that gave Woking a look in, as McAllister's marker went A.W.O.L. in the very final minute of injury time at the end of the first half. A draw was not such a bad result though, as many other teams hopeful of the play offs drew also. Only Exeter and Grays in the top nine won today.

HUFC: Brown, Green, Mkandawire, James, Jeannin, Purdie, Stanley, King, Taylor, Williams, Fleetwood. Subs: Beckwith, Mawson, Pitman, Nicolau, Stansfield.

WFC: Jalal, Jackson, Nethercott, Hutchinson, MacDonald, Murray, Smith, Evans, Liam Cockerill, McAllister , Ferguson. Subs: El-Salahi, Davies, Sam Cockerill, Oyedele, Blackman.

Morecambe v Hereford United, 4 April 2006-. Report by Ex Landlord

Bulls earn deserved point at Morecambe

Hereford twice came from behind at Christie Park on Tuesday night to come away with a well-earned point against play-off chasing Morecambe and arguably did enough to claim all three. Graham Turner implemented some "squad rotation" changes as well as replacing the injured Tony James with Dean Beckwith. Both Andy Williams and Stuart Fleetwood were rested and took their places on the bench to provide starts for Stansfield and Danny Carey-Bertram while Jamie Pitman came in for Robbie King.This was the first time since the game at Scarborough in January that Adam and DCB had started together.

The early exchanges gave no indication of the misfortune that was to hit Hereford in the third minute.A hopeful punt forward from the Morecambe midfield brought Wayne Brown into action to clear the ball under pressure to Jamie Pitman who hooked the ball away over his shoulder.The ball struck the referee and fell to Michael Twiss who coolly lobbed the ball into the net passed the stranded Brown to give the Shrimps a lucky lead. Hereford soon showed attacking intentions of their own when Craig Stanley put Daryl Taylor in but the Walsall loanee shot weakly and the ball was cleared by Morecambe's Garry Hunter. On 7 minutes Stanley himself fired just over from 25 yards having been supplied by Purdie and a minute later a second Stanley effort from just outside the box flew inches over when Taylor's miss-hit effort fell at his feet. The Morecambe midfield were closing down quickly and Twiss received a yellow card following his third foul in just five minutes.

While Morecambe looked more comfortable in possession, The Bulls were having their share of chances with Jeannin and Stansfield both going close. At the other end, the right sided Gary Thompson was giving Jeannin a tough time with his pacey play and provided a good chance for Carlton whose crisp shot was well held by Brown. On the half hour mark Jeannin broke forward to feed the influential Rob Purdie who was scythed down by Thompson but the resulting free kick was headed clear. Jeannin was carded a little harshly when Twiss ran across his path and the tangle of legs saw the Morecambe player go down.

The half finished with the hard running Stansfield winning a corner which was cleared by 'keeper Drench HT Morecambe 1 Hereford 0.

Play recommenced without the use of substitutions and United were quickly on the attack with Taylor moving at pace down the wing only to be felled by a somewhat "rustic" challenge from full back Michael Howard.The resulting low free kick from Jeannin was almost turned in by DCB. However, the Hereford striker did not have to wait long before he converted the next chance. The advancing Ryan Green delivered the ball deep into the host's goalmouth and Carey-Bertram was on hand to force the ball home and level the score on forty nine minutes.

Unfortunately, the Shrimps response was to regain the lead almost from the restart. Thompson swung in a cross from the right and as the central throng challenged in the air, the ball fell to Carlton who fired in from six yards. Shortly afterwards a rare Taylor cross was hacked away for a corner by Kempson and the resultant flag kick by Taylor saw the winger slice the ball behind for a goal kick. Craig Stanley was on the receiving end of a nasty tackle from Carlton who entered the referee's little book for his effort. Twenty minutes into the second period, the clearly tiring Stansfield was replaced with Stuart Fleetwood and the largely ineffective Taylor made way for Andy Williams who assumed the role of right midfield. Williams was swiftly into the action when he picked the ball on the halfway line and ran powerfully at the Shrimps defence before cutting inside to fire in a shot which shaved the crossbar.

Both Williams and Rob Purdie were causing problems for Morecambe with their direct attacking wing play and Curtis was fortunate not to see yellow when he dumped Williams on his backside. Jeannin's free kick only just avoided Mkandawire's outstretched foot as the classy centre back joined the attack. The Bulls were now dictating the game with Rob Purdie having his best attacking game for some time. Pitman and Stanley took over the central area as Morecambe were forced to defend deeper and looked to rely on breakaways. This allowed space for Jeannin and Green to push forward and it was this increased pressure which forced a free kick just outside the Shrimps penalty area on 79 minutes. Jeannin, Purdie and Fleetwood all lined up for the kick but it looked like Fleetwood who curled the ball towards the goal. The 'keeper, Steve Drench, managed to tip the ball against the upright but Carey-Bertram was on hand to nod the rebound over the line for the equalizer.

Although the Shrimps management threw on both Dodgson and Barlow for Curtis and Carlton with ten minutes to go, it was Hereford who finished the stronger. DCB might have got his hat trick and the winning goal with 5 minutes remaining when Rob Purdie again produced a delightful through ball which he flicked on, only to see it blocked on the line. Ryan Green appeared to take a knock and was replaced by Simon Travis for the last few minutes as United collected their one point reward following the long trip north.

With Daryl Taylor making the final appearance of his loan period, it was interesting to see the dangerous Williams used on the right side when Taylor was withdrawn. Is this a sign?

Morecambe:- Drench, Howard, Twiss, Curtis (Dodgson 80), Thompson, Kempson, Blackburn, Carlton (Barlow 80), Hunter, Brannan, McClachlan. Subs not used Robinson, Kelly, Rigoglioso.

HUFC:- Brown, Green (Travis 86), Mkandawire, Beckwith, Jeannin, Purdie, Pitman, Stanley, Taylor(Williams 65), Carey-Bertram, Stansfield (Fleetwood 65). Subs not used Mawson, King

My MOTM – Rob Purdie
Attendance 1699 (85/100 HUFC)

Hereford United v Dagenham & Redbridge, 8 April 2006. Report by Brian Goodwin

United stutter at home again

Hereford United faced Dagenham & Redbridge at Edgar Street this afternoon as they looked to take another step towards finalising their place in the play-offs for a third season running. They had to do without Ryan Green who missed out through injury and, in the only other change from the side that started against Morecambe, Adam Stansfield

Hereford United v Dagenham and Redbridge.
Hereford United's Alex Jeannin and Rob Purdie celebrate Purdie's goal from the penalty spot.

was demoted to the bench, meaning Andy Williams partnered Danny Carey-Bertram in attack.

United dominated what was a fairly uneventful first half, and began well when Craig Stanley headed into the arms of Tony Roberts at the far post, following Alex Jeannin's free kick from the right. Dean Beckwith should have done better when he headed the Frenchman's corner wide from a central

Hereford United v Dagenham and Redbridge.
Hereford midfielder Craig Stanley just loses out to Dagenham captain Tim Cole.

position with seven minutes gone, then Williams volleyed towards goal from twenty five yards, but his effort didn't really trouble Roberts in goal for the visitors.

Hereford were again most threatening in the air, and it took a sliced clearance that went out for a corner to deny Tamika Mkandawire, who'd headed Stanley's flick on header, towards goal. Daryl Taylor finally got the better of his man with little more than ten minutes of the first half remaining, after several attempts, and cut back to Jamie Pitman for Hereford's best opening of the half. However Pitman's first time shot flashed wide of the near post. Wayne Brown was forced into his first save of the afternoon in the closing stages of the half when he went down well to his right to claim a header from Sam Saunders.

Saunders again went close for The Daggers just after the restart, but headed over this time before The Bulls put together their best move of the match. Simon Travis played the ball down the flank to Taylor, who returned the pass having advanced past his marker, Scott Griffiths, and into the box. Travis crossed to the far post where Stanley headed the ball back across goal, as the angle was too tight to shoot from. The ball was then cleared behind for the first of four corners in succession. A minute later, Rob Purdie went close when he hit Jeannin's throw in first time, but his shot flew into the side netting.

With seventy four minutes gone, The Daggers made a double change and United replaced Pitman with Stuart Fleetwood, allowing Williams to move to the left flank, and Fleetwood was immediately in the action. Williams crossed from the left and, had it not been for a great last-ditch touch on by Anwar Uddin, Fleetwood would have been on cue to tap home. However, Fleetwood was on the end of the resulting corner with his head, which then hit Saunders, who was adjudged by the referee to have handballed, and a penalty was given. Purdie stepped up calmly, and placed the

Hereford United v Dagenham and Redbridge.
FOILED... Hereford's Tamika Mkandawire looks on as Daggers defender Chris Moore clears from a corner.

ball right into the corner, just beyond the reach of Roberts, who'd guessed correctly and dived to his right.

As the visitors has very rarely threatened, it looked as though the single goal would be enough to claim the three points for Hereford, but referee R. Fletcher had other ideas. Griffiths made his way into the United box having managed to hold off Beckwith, but Brown was out to meet him and, seemingly fairly, smothered the ball at his feet. Fletcher though, blew up and pointed to the spot, leaving some very baffled faces on and off the pitch. Glenn Southam didn't mind though, as he stepped up and tucked the ball away to Brown's left for the equaliser.

Hereford United v Dagenham and Redbridge.
GOAL... Rob Purdie scores the penalty.

Graham Turner introduced Adam Stansfield for Taylor immediately, with five minutes to go, but to no result. The Dagger's sub Paul Benson went closest to a winner, as he fought off Beckwith, but shot narrowly wide of the far post.

The point, which was probably a fair result in a lacklustre game, means Hereford stay in second place, with a five point advantage over Halifax – who are in third with a game in hand. The attendance of 2,561, including 68 away fans, was the highest of the day.

HUFC: Brown, Travis, Mkandawire, Beckwith, Jeannin, Purdie, Stanley, Pitman, Taylor, Carey-Bertram, Williams. Subs: Mawson, Gwynne, King, Fleetwood, Stansfield.

D&RFC: Roberts, Blackett, Cole, Uddin, Foster , Saunders, Southam, Bruce, Griffiths, Moore, Mackail-Smith. Subs: Vickers, Lettejallon, Benson, Akurang, Hogan.

One Foot in the Play Offs

Hereford United all but secured their place in the play offs for a third successive season following their 1-0 victory at Moss Lane this afternoon, against Altrincham. Morecambe were 3-0 victors at Tamworth, meaning, at the worst, Hereford can only finish 6th on goal difference. A victory on Monday, against Tamworth, for the Bulls would finalise their position in the top five.

United made a few changes from the draw with Dagenham last weekend – the only forced one was the replacement of Daryl Taylor on the right by Andy Williams, as the former's loan spell has ended. Andy Ferrell was back in the middle in place of Jamie Pitman and Stuart Fleetwood was back in the starting line up in place of Adam Stansfield, who was benched. There were returns from injury, but only to the subs bench, for Guy Ipoua and Nicky Nicolau.

Hereford started brightly with Rob Purdie causing plenty of problems on the left, and it was his dangerous early cross that was clawed away by 'keeper Stuart Coburn. Ferrell had fired off target in the sixth minute before Fleetwood should have broken the deadlock. United had broke well down the right, where they were to enjoy much success in the first half, and Simon Travis delivered a cross for Fleetwood, but his first time effort was somehow tipped onto the cross bar by Coburn.

Stanley had an even better chance to open the scoring just before the half hour mark, after another fast attack down the right caused problems for the Alty defence. This time it was Williams who was the creator, but Stanley volleyed just wide from a central position, from around twelve yards out.

United continued to dominate after the break, but still struggled to make Coburn work that hard in the Alty goal. The Bulls enjoyed much possession around the box and were very rarely threatened at the back for the opening stages of the second half, but the nearest to a shot on goal came through Stanley, whose effort from outside of the box was deflected to safety.

Colin Little had Alty's first real effort at goal when he headed over before Fleetwood finally made a break through in the sixty fourth minute. The Robins had squandered possession in the middle and Ferrell managed to thread an inch-perfect pass, just beyond the toes of the impressive Gary Talbot, and into the path of Fleetwood's run. He made no mistake when faced by the on rushing Coburn, as he fired powerfully into the back of the net.

United took their foot off the gas once they'd got the goal, and Altrincham did come into the game a bit. However, the Bulls almost doubled the lead when an Alex Jeannin corner found Danny Carey-Bertram at the far post, but his first time shot was blocked on the line. Tamika Mkandawire was first to the rebound, but his shot was deflected behind for a corner. Williams also had a good chance, but he was just beaten to a cross from man of the match Purdie, by the flying Coburn.

Substitute Kieran Lugsden shot narrowly wide as the hosts tried to salvage a point before Guy Ipoua replaced Williams in the eighty fourth minute. Hereford had one final chance before Ipoua's introduction, and it was Ferrell, who'd created the first goal, who went close. Williams received the ball into his feet, fifteen yards out with his back to goal, and touched the ball onto Ferrell who met it first time with a thunderous effort, that whistled just wide of the top corner.

It was, again, not the best performance from United but it is points that matter at this stage of the season. However, Hereford did look solid at the back and a little more fluency and pace to their game would most probably do them a world of good. Another positive for the Hereford following in the crowd of 1,251 was the return of Ipoua. The Bulls will want to have everyone fit and available for their inevitable play off campaign.

HUFC: Brown, Travis, Beckwith, Mkandawire, Jeannin, Purdie, Ferrell, Stanley, Williams, Carey-Bertram, Fleetwood. Subs: Mawson, Pitman, Nicolau, Stansfield, Ipoua.

AFC: Coburn, Aspinall, Talbot, Band, Scott, Potts, Murphy, Peyton, Chalmers, Little, Thornley. Subs: McFadden, Adams, Lugsden, Munroe, Norton

Hereford United v Tamworth, 17 April 2006. Report by Brian Goodwin

Carey-Bertram Bags Bulls Play Off Place

Hereford United claimed the victory that they needed to secure their play off place for the third successive season with a narrow 1-0 victory at home against strugglers Tamworth, who sit just one point out of the relegation zone now, with all three teams below them in the table having a game or more in hand on them.

Changes were inevitably made as The Bulls took to the field for the second time in three days. Wayne Brown, Craig Stanley and Andy Williams all dropped to the bench and Craig Mawson, Jamie Pitman and Nicky Nicolau took their places in what was the same sixteen as named against Altrincham.

The Lambs enjoyed the early efforts at goal, but ex-Bull Daniel Davidson scuffed his shot wide before former English and Scottish Premiership attacker Tommy Johnson stung the hands of Mawson with a powerful effort from

Hereford v Tamworth

Hereford United's Tamika Mkandawire beats Tamworth defender Matt Redmile to get a header in on goal.

Hereford v Tamworth
Tamworth defender Michael Tuohy clears a Hereford corner.

twenty yards. The visitors had to make a change after just eighteen minutes as Alan Neilson limped off injured, and was replaced by Nathan Jackson.

United, who'd enjoyed most of the possession but not the chances, first threatened through a corner from Rob Purdie, which was taken off the head of Dean Beckwith by a defender for another corner. The second corner was half cleared to Andy Ferrell, who lofted the ball back into the box where Tamika Mkandawire found himself ahead of the defence, who were calling for an offside that never came, but the Malawian's header was straight at 'keeper Sean Bowles.

Purdie picked a brilliant pass from deep inside his own half that went route one over the defence and into the path of Carey-Bertram – who was only to be denied by a fantastic recovering challenge by Adie Smith. Johnson was the next player to leave the field early for the visitors, as he was removed eight minutes before the break to make way for Tristan Whitman. The former Doncaster attacker was straight into the action and almost broke the deadlock with a rocket of a shot that curled towards the far post, and flashed just inches wide.

Both sides came out unchanged for the second half, but it was obvious that great improvements was needed by both. It came as well, with United becoming more ambitious and gambling a bit more in attack – something which Tamworth didn't handle too well, and found themselves boxed in their own half for huge periods of the half. Carey-Bertram had already signalled intention, when he worked himself an opening, but fired into the arms of Bowles, before he managed to get the decisive goal after fifty eight minutes. Ferrell was, like against Altrincham, the creator as he threaded a superbly weighted through ball into Carey-

Hereford United v Tamworth.
Tamworth 'keeper collects Sean Bowles collects a cross watched by Hereford forwards Andy Williams and Adam Stansfield.

Hereford v Tamworth
Hereford United's Danny Carey-Bertram (right) celebrates his goal against Tamworth with team mates Simon Travis and Andy Williams.

Bertram's path. The striker made no mistake as he smashed the ball, first time, beyond the reach of the advancing goalie.

Tamworth replied by finally getting some men forward, but Graham Ward's long range strike was the closest they came until injury time at the end of the game. Hereford, on the other hand, went from strength to strength, boosted by the goal and then by the introduction of Andy Williams, who took Nicky Nicolau's place. At the same time, with sixty five minutes on the clock, Stuart Fleetwood was withdrawn for Adam Stansfield.

Carey-Bertram, who now has eight Conference goals for this season, was obviously brimming with confidence as he attempted to lob Bowles from all of thirty five yards, but the ball fell just over the cross bar, before Williams almost netted a scorcher. Alex Jeannin picked out the youngster with an inch perfect cross field pass that Williams took inside his man before firing a left footed shot that required a brilliant tip over the bar to prevent The Bulls from doubling their advantage.

Mkandawire forced another save from Bowles, before Williams again went close but volleyed a Jeannin corner wide at the far post. Carey-Bertram had another chance when Bowles sliced a clearance but, having beaten his marker, Carey-Bertram volleyed wildly and his shot was well off the mark. With little more than five minutes left, Guy Ipoua was introduced, and the goal scorer made way. Ipoua was immediately involved, as he held up play for Pitman to release Stansfield down the right, but his low cross evaded both Ferrell and Purdie who awaited unmarked at the far post.

The three minutes of injury time held plenty of incident also, as Tamworth could have, and probably should have, equalised, before United almost sealed the win. Substitute Bob Taylor was on the end of a high ball that had beaten the Hereford defence (about the only thing that did in the whole game) but his first time effort flew just inches over the cross bar. Williams had the chance at the other end, which he created for himself following a neat spin and run, but his shot was deflected behind. Still there was time for make-shift striker Matt Redmile to head straight at Mawson before the referee bought the game to a close.

Despite Hereford's constant domination, the term "a game of two halves" was very fitting, as the first half was, from both teams, very poor. It lacked pace from both, with Tamworth just stopping Hereford from going forward with a blockade of nine or ten players, while the hosts were happy enough to just knock the ball about themselves. Luckily for the crowd of 2,809, which included 185 away fans, Hereford decided to throw some more players forwards in the second half, making the game far more entertaining – and it paid off, as United cemented their place in the top five in the Conference.

HUFC: Mawson, Travis, Beckwith, Mkandawire, Jeannin, Nicolau, Pitman, Ferrell, Purdie, Carey-Bertram, Fleetwood. Subs: Mawson, Stanley, Stansfield, Williams, Ipoua.

TFC: Bowles, Redmile, Folkes, Smith, Roma, Ward, Neilson, Storer, Touhy, Davidson, Johnson. Subs: Dryden, Gayle, Taylor, Whitman, Jackson.

Hereford United v Southport, 22 April 2006. Report by Brian Goodwin

Bulls Take It Easy Again

It was the same story as the two games over the Easter period as Hereford United took on Southport, fighting for survival at the bottom of the Conference, at Edgar Street this afternoon. That was the case, until the last minute of normal time when a breakaway goal changed things.

Hereford made just two changes from the side that started against Tamworth last Monday, with Andy Williams returning to the starting eleven at the expense of Nicky Nicolau and Wayne Brown replacing Craig Mawson. It seemed a good move as United started brightly and attacked well from the start, particularly down the right where Williams was playing. Craig Stanley picked out Rob Purdie with a ball to the left flank as The Bulls tried to gain an early advantage.

Hereford United v Southport
Adam Stansfield puts Hereford United 1-0 up against Southport.

Hereford United v Southport
Hereford United 'keeper Wayne Brown is well beaten as Liam Blakeman's equaliser rockets into the net.

Purdie slipped a ball into the run of Stuart Fleetwood, who was denied from a tight angle by 'keeper Steve Dickinson.

Andy Ferrell gifted the ball to Carl Baker at the other end, but his low drive was easily gathered by Brown before Hereford were on the attack again. Danny Carey-Bertram had touched the ball back to Ferrell, who then spread play to the left where Alex Jeannin skipped past a challenge before delivering an inviting cross to the far post. Fleetwood though, was just underneath the cross and it was headed behind for a corner.

Hereford thought they'd taken the lead midway through the half, but a dubious decision by the referee meant the scores stayed level. Ferrell was felled thirty yards out by a rash challenge, which the referee let go. The ball had broken to Carey-Bertram, who had turned towards goal and then fired a low shot into the bottom corner from the edge of the box. The whistle had already been blown though by the time the ball had netted, and the referee brought play back for a free kick for the foul on Ferrell – which he originally let go. If he'd played advantage, it was a baffling decision to say the least, as Hereford obviously had an advantage.

This seemed to give the Sandgrounders a boost and they had the best chances of the rest of the half. Firstly, after Tamika Mkandawire had slipped, Dean Beckwith was left to deal with two attacker and the ball was played to Steve Daly, but his effort rebounded away off the post. Then, on the stroke of half time, defender Gary Brabin headed inches over from a corner kick.

Graham Turner introduced Adam Stansfield at the break in the place of Carey-Bertram, and then minutes after Port made a change as the injured Daly was replaced by Neil Robinson. Stansfield was quick to get an effort in when he latched onto a flick on by Fleetwood, but he blazed his effort well wide before Stansfield was blocked off in the box following some patient build up play. Brabin, at the other end, drilled a free kick wide of the mark, albeit via a deflection.

Hereford United v Southport
Adam Stansfield celebrates his goal with team mates as Southport 'keeper Steve Dickinson and defender Gary Brabin look less than impressed.

Hereford United v Southport.
Hereford players Craig Stanley and Alex Jeannin complain to referee Mr Shoebridge after he disallowed Danny Carey-Bertram's goal and awarded a free kick to Hereford instead!

Jamie Pitman was introduced in place of Fleetwood and Williams, who had been quiet so far, moved alongside Stansfield in attack. This meant that Ferrell, seemingly, moved to the left and Stanley to the right, leaving Purdie to play in the centre. It took a while, but the change seemed to pay off as Hereford took the lead with fourteen minutes left. United pressed around their opponents box before Ferrell slipped a ball wide to Simon Travis who had some space. His first time cross to the near post was met with a delightful header from Stansfield that glanced into the far bottom corner, much to the relief of the somewhat frustrated home fans in a crowd 2,547.

Southport had to come out and attack after the goal and began to show more intent going forward and even more aggression in the tackles. Baker triggered a mass brawl as he left the studs showing in a tackle against Brown and was booked once everyone had calmed down. Then with about ten minutes left, Guy Ipoua was subbed on in place of Williams, and the Cameroonian showed some nice touches in his short spell on the pitch. Purdie, who was again Hereford's most creative player, especially when playing in a central position, and man of the match, saw a shot deflected shot go wide before Southport grabbed a late equaliser.

A long ball from the middle of the park picked out Robinson, making a break down the left, and he held up the ball until Blakeman arrived on the edge of the box. Blakeman jinked inside and then unleashed an unstoppable shot into the far top corner, much to the delight of the travelling 182 supporters.

The game plan for The Whites was again evident – to do just enough to win the game, without sustaining any injuries or picking up too many cards, and it almost worked for a third game in a row, until a breakaway goal in the final minute. It was poor to watch for the most apart, but not too many people will be complaining if this game plan pays off come the end of the play offs.

HUFC: Brown, Travis, Mkandawire, Beckwith, Jeannin, Purdie, Stanley, Ferrell, Williams, Carey-Bertram, Fleetwood. Subs: Pitman, Nicolau, Mawson, Stansfield, Ipoua

York City v Hereford United, 29 April 2006. Report by Brian Goodwin

Runners up for third successive season

Hereford United secured their almost traditional second place in the Conference this afternoon with a 3-1 victory away at York City. It was the first time that The Bulls have scored three goals away from home in the league this season, and continued their superb run that has seen them go unbeaten in the Conference on their travels since the 7th of October.

Changes were made in the Hereford side as Danny Carey-Bertram missed out through injury and Ryan Green returned. Simon Travis played on the right of midfield in front of

Green, who played at right back. It took Hereford a while to get into their stride, and York enjoyed the earliest of the chances. Travis blocked an early shot, forcing a corner before Dean Beckwith had to get in the way of a shot from Andy Bishop, who won another corner for the hosts. It was a third corner from which The Minstermen came closest, as the ball fell to Neal Bishop who fired first time, but Wayne Brown was equal to it.

Hereford were not as wasteful with their chances, and took the lead following their first effort on goal after thirteen minutes. Craig Stanley won a free kick just outside the box that Alex Jeannin fired low and hard. The goalkeeper Chris Porter parried the ball away, but only into the path of Andy Williams, who fired low into the far corner from close range. United got themselves into the game as York's early spirits had been dampened but failed to create another decent chance until the thirty fifth minute – when they scored again!

Some good passing in the midfield managed to release Travis in space on the right flank, and he had time to cross into the middle where Andy Williams challenged Porter for the ball. Neither won it clearly and it rolled out to the far post where Rob Purdie was on hand to tuck in a second for The Bulls. Purdie had an opportunity for a second before the break but, after Williams had flicked on a ball from Jeannin, his low shot was tame and no trouble for Porter.

York came out for the restart with renewed optimism. Clayton Donaldson made his way down the right before centring for Joe O'Neill but Brown again saved, however he couldn't deny City on fifty seven minutes. A free kick from Mark Convery was headed straight into the path of Andy Bishop, who stole in to head home from five yards, for his 25th goal of the season. City went on to have a strong period, but couldn't find the equaliser.

Hereford's Williams had a shot blocked before Adam Stansfield should have restored the two goal advantage, with Travis once again the supplier, when the striker couldn't get a cross from under his feet, with a clear view on goal inside the six yard box. Ferrell forced the save of the game out of Porter from twenty five yards with a well hit shot before Tamika Mkandawire almost scored, but his header was just inches off target. Soon after this, Graham Turner made two changes replacing both his strikers in the eighty second minute. Stuart Fleetwood and Guy Ipoua were introduced but it was York who went closest to scoring again.

This time it took a header off the line by Stanley, following a free kick, and a tip over from Brown to deny the hosts. The resulting corner caused more problems, causing a mass scramble in the goal mouth, in which it looked as though York may have netted twice before the ball went wide for a goal kick. Hereford survived the late storm though and went on to score a third in the final minute from substitute Ipoua. The move started with Brown who sent a long ball wide to Green on the right, and the Welshman then found his fellow country man Fleetwood. The striker ran at goal before poking the ball onto Purdie, who set up Ipoua with a low ball across the goal leaving the Cameroonian to net from close range, much to the delight, and relief, of the 329 Hereford fans in a crowd of 2,755.

So it's second again for Hereford and they will now face Morecambe in the play offs. The performance today was much better than those seen recently, and will have given encouragement both to the team and supporters.

HUFC: Brown, Green, Beckwith, Mkandawire, Jeannin, Purdie, Stanley, Ferrell, Travis, Williams, Stansfield. Subs: Pitman, Mawson, Nicolau, Ipoua, Fleetwood.

YCFC: Porter, Thomas, McGurk, Dudgeon, Peat, Panther, O'Neill, Neil Bishop, Dunning, Donaldson, Andy Bishop. Subs: Hotte, Reid, Convery, Kamara, Merris.

It's one all at half time

Hereford United came away from Christie Park with a one all draw in the first leg of the play off semi finals against Morecambe this evening. It is the third time in as many seasons that The Bulls have earned an away draw before having to settle the match at Edgar Street, with the first leg effectively meaning nothing at all.

Graham Turner decided to play the same team that defeated York City last weekend, meaning Adam Stansfield and Andy Williams led the front line; and it was the latter who volleyed a Simon Travis cross wide of the near post in United's opening attack. Michael Twiss had seen a volley saved by Wayne Brown before the hosts broke the deadlock, with Twiss the supplier. Though there was some controversy about the goal, as Gary Thompson appeared to quite blatantly pushed Alex Jeannin in the back, forcing a corner for Morecambe. Twiss delivered to the far post, out of the reach of Brown, and onto the head of the flying Jim Bentley.

It had taken twenty two minutes for the first goal, and it was just a few minutes later when Rob Purdie almost grabbed the second. Stansfield found a pass for Purdie in behind the defence, but he fired low and wide of the near post from a tight angle. Wayne Curtis then broke for The Shrimpers, played a one-two, and then shot hard towards the near post, where Brown turned the ball around the post. United couldn't quite force an equaliser before the break, but went close following a counter attack led by Purdie and then Jeannin, who crossed for Williams but United gained just a corner, which Stansfield headed over.

United were unchanged for the second half in personnel, but in performance there was every change as they began to completely dominate. Craig Stanley was played in on goal by Stansfield, but was forced slightly wide and then saw his shot saved by Steven Drench, and Ferrell's follow up shot was saved as United signalled their intentions from the off. However, United were struggling to create all that much in the way of real chances, they were dominating play, until Bentley almost doubled the lead with a repeated corner move to the far post.

It was nine minutes into the second half though, when a vital decision by the man in the middle put Hereford back on level terms. Fraser McLachlan appeared to clear the ball behind for a corner when the referee strangely pointed to the penalty spot, though many Hereford fans behind the goal thought he'd given a goal kick. Delighted, as well as shocked, they were when they realised that Purdie had a chance to level things up – which he did, shooting low into the corner, to the 'keepers right.

Wild celebrations by the 1,100 + travelling army (in a crowd of 5,208) followed, as well as an onslaught from the team. Purdie shot over from outside the box, before Stanley fired just wide having robbed the ball in the middle, in a period when both he and Purdie excelled. Stanley headed inches wide of the far post minutes later and then Purdie picked out Travis on the right, who crossed for Williams, but his header was inches over the bar.

United couldn't find a second, and another dubious decision actually kept them in the game as Twiss had a goal, totally against the run of play, ruled out by the linesman for offside. Thompson then flashed a shot across the goal as Morecambe came back into things. Turner realised the need for changes after this, and bought Guy Ipoua and Stuart Fleetwood on, with little more than five minutes to go, to little avail.

The two sides will meet again on Thursday to decide the tie, which is finely balanced between two sides who have had three close encounters this season. If the form books are anything to go by, which they usually are not, then perhaps United have the upper hand, as Morecambe have a far better home record than away record. Then again, Hereford seem to do fair better away from home than at Edgar Street.

HUFC: Brown, Green, Mkandawire, Beckwith, Jeannin, Purdie, Stanley, Ferrell, Travis, Stansfield, Williams. Subs: Mawson, Pitman, Carey-Bertram, Ipoua, Fleetwood.

Hereford United v Morecambe, 11 May 2006. Report by Brian Goodwin

Guy's the magic match winner

Finally! They've done it! It's taken three attempts, but Hereford United are through to the Conference play off final for the first time! But they made hard work of it and took the lead three times in total, in an enthralling second leg encounter at Edgar Street, with Morecambe the visitors.

Unchanged from the first leg were The Bulls, and they began where they left off in the second half from the first leg, which finished 1-1. United were dominant from the start and with just six minutes on the clock Tamika Mkandawire sent the home crowd into raptures, with a fantastic header from Alex Jeannin's corner. The Frenchman though, turned from hero to villain in minutes as Morecambe went down the other end a minute later and Jeannin blatantly fouled in the area, and Wayne Curtis equalised from the penalty spot.

United, with the huge home vocal support behind them all the way, didn't dwell on it

Hereford United v Morecambe Play Off Semi Final
GOAL... Tamika Mkandawire heads Hereford into an early lead.

Hereford United v Morecambe Play Off Semi Final
Hereford players celebrate Tamika Mkandawire's goal.

Hereford United v Morecambe Play Off Semi Final
GOAL... Tamika Mkandawire celebrates his goal with team mate Rob Purdie.

however, and continued to dominate, and just five minutes later local lad Andy Williams scored a fantastic goal. Adam Stansfield raced away down the left before nipping a ball inside to Rob Purdie. Purdie played the ball into the feet of Williams who, with his back to goal and a defender behind him, somehow managed to turn and fire, all in one motion, into the bottom corner of the net leaving 'keeper Steven Drench stranded.

Minutes later, the visitors were almost on level terms again when Mkandawire headed a long ball straight into the path of the oh-so-dangerous Michael Twiss, and his first time shot flew inches wide of Wayne Brown's post. Simon Travis then went close for Hereford, as he stung the hands of Drench with a drive from twenty-five yards, before he crossed for Williams, but his header was easy for the loanee 'keeper. Morecambe enjoyed a good spell of play for around ten minutes before half time, but they couldn't make anything of it. Hereford though, finished the half more brightly, and went in at the break 2-1 up.

The Shrimpers were to enjoy another good spell after the interval, not because of their renewed approach after the restart, but because United gave them much more time on the ball in the middle. And Hereford paid the price for this. With eight minutes of the half gone Danny Carlton broke in behind the Bull's back line, forced a save from Brown at

TENSION TO TRIUMPH...
Hereford United supporters witness their team drawing with Morecambe.

TENSION TO TRIUMPH...
Hereford United supporters witness their team winning against Morecambe.

Jubilant Hereford fans celebrate their teams success at the end of the game.

Hereford United v Morecambe Play off semi final.
Hereford United's Simon Travis finds his shot closed down quickly by two Morecambe defenders.

Hereford United v Morecambe Play Off Semi Final
Hereford's Andy Williams celebrates his goal with team mate Craig Stanley to delight of the Bulls fans.

a tight angle, but the ball fell into the path of Twiss who netted from a central position.

Hereford should have equalised almost immediately, but first the tenacious Andy Ferrell was denied, following Williams' cross, by a great save at the far post and then, with Drench stranded but a crowd of players to avoid, Purdie struck the foot of the post from the edge of the box before the ball was put behind. Morecambe took control of the game once again for a period in a second half that they had the better of, and so Graham Turner made a double change, on seventy three minutes, with Stansfield and Jeannin – who had a poor game in all honesty – making way for Stuart Fleetwood and Jamie Pitman. Simon Travis went to left back.

Curtis almost grabbed an astonishing second, but his thunderbolt from thirty yards flashed just inches over the bar, and then the man of the moment, Guy Ipoua, was introduced with eight minutes remaining. However, he didn't make his impact until the

Hereford United v Morecambe Play Off Semi Final
TENSE... John Trewick and Graham Turner.

game had gone into extra time, having finished 2-2 after ninety minutes.

The first half of extra time saw chances for both and Brown had to pull off a good low save from Gary Thompson while Purdie, at the other end, almost stole in as the Morecambe defence left a long ball go through to Drench. In the second half, Twiss forced Brown into another good low save, shooting from the left early on, before Ipoua produced the magic.

Hereford United v Morecambe Play Off Semi Final
FLYING THE FLAG... Hereford supporter Sharon Wild joined thousands of others to cheer their team into the play off final.

Hereford United v Morecambe Play Off Semi Final
GOALLLLLLLLLLLLLL... Hereford forward Guy Ipoua hits the winner!

Hereford United v Morecambe Play Off Semi Final
CHARGING BULL... Hereford's Guy Ipoua races towards the bench after scoring the winner against Morecambe. With Ipoua are team mates Andy Ferrell, Craig Stanley and Rob Purdie.

Hereford United v Morecambe Play Off Semi Final
Hereford United's Alex Jeannin and Guy Ipoua celebrate at the end of the game.

He raced on to, yes actually ran, a long ball and managed to beat two defenders to the ball and knock it on for himself with his head, before it bounced at a perfect height for him to smash stunningly, from around twelve yards out to the right of the box, into the far top corner of the net, causing scenes of mayhem in the stands among the Hereford fans in a crowd of 6,278 (including 528 away fans).

Hereford played out the rest of the half with their backs to the wall, pretty much, but did it well with the full backing of the Hereford

Hereford United v Morecambe Play Off Semi Final

Hereford United defender Ryan Green manages to make it to the dressing room as jubilant fans invade Edgar Street after the play off victory against Morecambe. Little did Green know but he was to become an even bigger hero in the final!

faithful. Fleetwood had a good chance on the break to double the advantage when Purdie played him through, but he failed in rounding the goalie, not that it really mattered. The final whistle was blown after two minutes of injury time – cue mass celebrations, including a pitch invasion from the Hereford fans. Once the pitch was cleared, the players came back out for a lap of honour, and the delight was there to see for everyone!

It was, all in all, a very entertaining game helped by two sides who went out to play football and win. The atmosphere from both sets of fans was a credit to their clubs, and must have been a huge help to both teams. Now we need to do it all again in Leicester!

HUFC: Brown, Green, Mkandawire, Beckwith, Jeannin, Purdie, Ferrell, Stanley, Travis, Williams, Stansfield. Subs: Mawson, Pitman, Carey-Bertram, Fleetwood, Ipoua.

Hereford United v Morecambe Play Off Semi Final

IN FULL SONG… Jubilant Hereford United fans invade the Edgar Street pitch after beating Morecambe.

Hereford United v Morecambe Play Off Semi Final

Hereford United's Andy Williams celebrates after the Bulls beat Morecambe. Andy, a Hereford lad, scored the second goal as the Bulls beat Morecambe 3-2.

Hereford United v Morecambe Play Off Semi Final

Hereford United footballers and backroom staff celebrate the win over Morecambe.

Hereford United v Morecambe Play Off Semi Final

JUBILATION… As Hereford's players, management and backroom staff celebrate Guy Ipoua's winner against Morecambe.

The Bulls Are Back

After nine long years in non-league wilderness, Hereford United are back in the Football League. It took 120 minutes to find a winner, but eventually, after an enthralling and extremely tense encounter, The Bulls managed a 3-2 victory to send themselves up and to keep Halifax Town down. The Bulls are sure not to be in The Shaymen's good books, as it was Hereford who sent Town down from the league, though they have had a brief return since then.

With the game being played at the neutral venue of The Walkers Bowl, in Leicester, fans from both teams flooded to Leicester hours before kick off to soak up the pre-match atmosphere that built in the streets and pubs in the surrounding area. There appeared to be some friendly banter before the game, and the good manner seemed to carry on throughout the day with very little (if any) trouble evident.

It was the same side for Hereford that has been named for the previous three outings that emerged out of the tunnel to a huge welcome from the 9,000-10,000 Hereford fans in a crowd of 15,499. The opening stages of the tie were quite open, but it was Halifax who threatened first. Within the first couple of minutes Lewis Kileen had fired off target and he had another good effort, having collected a pass from strike-partner Ryan Sugden, drilled a low shot that Wayne Brown met well. Before Kileen's second effort, United's skipper Mkandawire was fortunate that his handball in the box went unnoticed.

The Shaymen, playing the ball better than their counter parts and looking far more

Hereford United v Halifax Town Conference Play Off Final.
Hereford United players line-up for the National anthem.

Hereford United v Halifax Town Conference Play Off Final.
Part of the estimated 10,000 Hereford United fans in The Walkers Stadium, Leicester.

dangerous going forward, almost stunned the Hereford fans when Danny Foster's shot skimmed off the top of the cross bar. However, Town weren't going to be wasteful any more and took full advantage on twenty seven minutes. United were reduced to ten men at the time, as Rob Purdie was receiving stitches to a head wound, when Kileen unleashed a brilliant first time effort that flew into the top left hand corner of Brown's goal from twenty odd yards.

Hereford United v Halifax Town
Conference Play Off Final.
Hereford goalkeeper Wayne Brown shares a joke with the mascot.

Hereford United v Halifax Town
Conference Play Off Final.
OH NO… Hereford go a goal down scored by Halifax forward Lewis Killeen despite a despairing dive from Bulls goalkeeper Wayne Brown.

Just minutes earlier, Craig Stanley had forced John Kennedy into his first real work of the afternoon, as Stanley's curling shot from twenty five yards required the fingertips of the 'keeper to force it over the crossbar. The goal though, had spurred United into action and seven minutes later the scores were level again. Mkandawire rallied the troops from the back, and raced out of defence with the ball, released it to the right, and continued his run all the way to the front post. Meanwhile, Adam Stansfield was racing down the flank and, with the skipper making a decoy run to the front post, youngster Andy Williams was left unmarked at the far post to meet the

Hereford United v Halifax Town Conference Play Off Final.
Hereford captain Tamika Mkandawire gets in a header from a corner watched by team mate Adam Stansfield.

ball with a diving header, that bounced off the surface before springing up, out of the reach of Kennedy, and just inside of the far post.

The Whites, boasting an all new white kit, went on to pose more problems for their opponents before the break, with Purdie having a close range header saved, but also being denied a penalty. Simon Travis raced into the box and seemed to be felled by Kennedy. The referee, in the eyes of many Hereford fans', has pointed to the spot, but he had actually given a goal kick.

United continued where they left off after the restart, and Stansfield almost put The Bulls in front. His mazy run bought him some space inside the box and he homed in on goal from the right but, with a clear sight on goal from just yards out, shot low to the near post, where Kennedy somehow managed to keep the ball out with his feet.

Hereford United v Halifax Town Conference Play Off Final.
OH YES… Hereford striker Andy Williams heads the Bulls level.

Hereford United v Halifax Town Conference Play Off Final.
Hereford's Rob Purdie goes down in the penalty area under a challenge from Halifax midfielder Greg Young.

It would also, again, appear that the referee was not on Hereford's side, much like the referee of the Aldershot play off semi final second leg of two years ago, when they were denied what was a clear-cut penalty just before the hour mark. Purdie had tore down the left wing, knocked the ball past his marker, and paced onto it, now inside the penalty area. Tyrone Thompson, the culprit of Purdie's sprint, then followed the former Leicester youth player and slid in from behind, catching Purdie on the calf muscles, but again – no penalty for the Bulls.

Still, The Bulls battled on and Stansfield had another glorious chance to put them in front. Travis supplied the cross to the far post, where Stansfield towered to meet it, but he diverted his header inches the wrong side of the post. At the other end Matt Doughty handed United a reminder when he hooked a shot wide of the far post from inside the box before the 65th minute introduction of one John Grant, formerly of Hereford United. Cue murmurs amongst some of the travelling Bulls about Grant, who had a hugely unsuccessful spell with them, being likely to come back to haunt them, while others taunted him.

And, of course, Grant silenced the critics by handing Halifax the lead with seventeen

Hereford United v Halifax Town
Conference Play Off Final.
IN FINE VOICE... Hereford United fans cheer the Bulls to victory.

Hereford United v Halifax Town
Conference Play Off Final.

Hereford United defender Tamika Mkandawire keeps a close eye on Halifax forward Ryan Sugden.

minutes remaining. Kileen was again involved as Halifax broke away down the left and he crossed for Grant, who put just the slightest of touches on the cross to divert it beyond the reach of the diving Brown. This was surely the final blow to Hereford – well it would have

Hereford United v Halifax Town
Conference Play Off Final.

Hereford midfielder Andy Ferrell is under pressure from Halifax counterpart Greg Young.

been to many Hereford sides we've seen over the years. But not to this one.

It took slightly longer for United to get back level this time, but just ten minutes had passed when Guy Ipoua netted a brilliant equaliser. He'd been on the pitch just five minutes, and had already caused Halifax problems when he rose up with the goal to send the game into extra time. Travis was the provider, crossing in from the right and Ipoua leapt above his man, stretched back his neck muscles, and got just enough power to put the ball above the reach of Kennedy and into the roof of the net in front of some now delirious Hereford fans.

The Bulls were again looking threatening straight after the restart of the extra time

Hereford United v Halifax Town
Conference Play Off Final.

Hereford forward Stuart Fleetwood rounds Halifax goalkeeper Jon Kennedy.

Hereford United v Halifax Town
Conference Play Off Final.

Hereford forward Adam Stansfield gets a header in on the Halifax goal.

period when Adam Stansfield lost his man before smashing the ball into the side netting, but with the net shaking, it would have appeared to some Hereford fans, located at the far end of the ground, that the ball had sneaked in side the near post. Not so. This was Stansfield's final contribution as he made way for the fresh legs of Stuart Fleetwood. This was Hereford's final change as Stanley had been replaced, having been suffering with cramp, at the end of normal time. Jamie Pitman was on to help the dogged Andy Ferrell who had excelled in the middle throughout.

Hereford United v Halifax Town
Conference Play Off Final.

Halifax defender Adam Quinn heads clear under pressure from Hereford's Tamika Mkandawire.

The second half of extra time saw the two teams attacking their own sets of fans, and, with three minutes of the second half gone, Ryan Green popped up with the third goal. After some good passing on the right, Green went to cross, before dragging the ball back onto his left foot, taking his marker out of the game. Green then, from just outside of the right hand side corner of the box, looped a left footed ball into the box, which evaded everyone, including Kennedy, and nestled into the top far corner of the goal. Whether he meant to shoot or cross, is another thing, but they all count, and that is all the jubilant United fans cared about. They'd taken the lead for the first time of the game.

There were still many more heart-stopping moments for The Bulls though, none more so than when Brown rushed out to the feet of Chris Senior, appearing to fell him, and the ball running out for, what in the end, despite appeals from Halifax for a penalty, was a goal kick. The worry wasn't over for Hereford though, as Brown remained on the deck. With all subs taken up, Ferrell had gone over the dugout and had started to put a 'keepers shirt on, when Brown struggled to his feet, and made eventually made a full recovery. The result though, was six minutes added on at the end, adding hugely to the tension being suffered by Hereford, who had waited so long for their return. The defence stood strong though, and Fleetwood, similarly to the game against Morecambe, had a great chance to make it 4-2 on the break. He outpaced the Halifax centre backs, rounded Kennedy, but his shot, which was good enough, was knocked off the line by Danny Bushell.

The final whistle finally, after what seemed an eternity, sounded, much to the delight of the Hereford fans. A phenomenal roar of

Hereford United v Halifax Town
Conference Play Off Final.

Hereford manager Graham Turner and assistant manager John Trewick.

Hereford United v Halifax Town
Conference Play Off Final.

GOAL... Ryan Green's superb strike beats Halifax goalkeeper Jon Kennedy to put The Bulls into the Football League.

Hereford United v Halifax Town
Conference Play Off Final.

Two Hereford supporters get behind their team.

Hereford United v Halifax Town
Conference Play Off Final.

GOAL... Ryan Green celebrates the winning goal with team mates and supporters.

delight, relief, and pure joy rang out from the Hereford end, and the celebrations began. And no doubt went on long into the early hours of the morning.

So Hereford United did it, but of course not the easy way. The game was a fantastic advert for the Conference, not only with a huge audience at the game, but being screened all over the world by Sky TV. Halifax have to take a huge amount of credit in making it such an entertaining final, in which both sets of fans experienced the extreme highs and lows of emotions. There had to be a winner though, and this was Hereford's turn, and no doubt they deserve it!

Hereford: Brown, Green, Beckwith, Mkandawire, Jeannin, Purdie, Stanley, Ferrell, Travis, Stansfield, Williams. Subs: Mawson, Pitman, Carey-Bertram, Fleetwood, Ipoua.

HTFC: Kennedy, Haslam, Quinn, Atherton, Young, Doughty, Foster, Thompson, Forrest, Sugden, Killeen. Subs: Bushell, Butler, Smikle, Senior, Grant

Hereford United v Halifax Town
Conference Play Off Final.

GET IN THERE... Hereford's Guy Ipoua equalises against Halifax.

Hereford United v Halifax Town
Conference Play Off Final.

WE'VE DONE IT... Hereford United manager Graham Turner turns to the crowd at the final whistle.

Hereford United v Halifax Town
Conference Play Off Final.

Hereford United striker Guy Ipoua holds the Conference Play Offs Bob Lord Trophy for the fans to touch.

Hereford United v Halifax Town
Conference Play Off Final.

Hereford United players celebrate promotion to the football league.

Hereford United v Halifax Town
Conference Play Off Final.

The champagne flows as Hereford United's players and coaching staff celebrate winning the Conference Play Off Final.

Hereford United v Halifax Town
Conference Play Off Final.

Hereford United defender Alex Jeannin congratulates manager Graham Turner.

Hereford United v Halifax Town Conference Play Off Final.

Hereford United's Guy Ipoua and Alex Jeannin are at the forefront of celebrations as they lift the Conference play off trophy.

Hereford United v Halifax Town
Conference Play Off Final.

CHAMPAGNE TIME... Hereford United manager Graham Turner proudly holds the Conference Play Offs Bob Lord Trophy.

Hereford United v Halifax Town
Conference Play Off Final.

A Hereford United fan gives Guy Ipoua a memento.

Hereford United v Halifax Town
Conference Play Off Final.

Hereford United's Guy Ipoua lifts the Conference Play Offs Bob Lord Trophy to show the Bulls fans.